"Mormonism is an experiential religion. People who want to argue with Mormons about the teachings and the texts of their religion may seriously miss the opportunity to communicate. David Rowe helps readers understand how Mormonism functions as a culture, a way of life, and even as a catalyst for burning-in-the-bosom moments of personal transcendence. Following Rowe's insights can help readers create points of deep personal contact with Mormons—and the potential for transformation."

David Neff, editor and vice president, *Christianity Today*

"For the past thirteen years, I have developed wonderful friendships with a small group of religion professors at Brigham Young University, all members of the Church of Jesus Christ of Latter-day Saints in good standing. Through extensive conversations I have learned firsthand what they actually believe and teach, what directions the church is heading in the twenty-first century, and how evangelical Christians are generally perceived in LDS circles. When people have asked me for the best resource available for how best to interact with LDS friends today with respect to religious topics, I have told them, 'The Bridges video series, produced by Salt Lake Seminary.' Now similar material is even more accessible in this book. A must read for all who care about this topic."

Craig L. Blomberg, distinguished professor of New Testament,
Denver Seminary

"Dave Rowe not only loves Mormons, he understands that an essential requirement of love is truth telling. He writes candidly about the appeal and burdens of Mormonism, the differences between it and historic Christianity, and our often counterproductive attempts to share our faith with Latter-day Saints. This book should be required reading for all who know Mormons or will soon know Mormons—which is to say, almost everyone. It is written with clarity, practicality, and most of all charity."

Donald McCullough, president, Salt Lake Theological Seminary

"This is a highly commendable example of the apostle Paul's directive to Timothy, his fellow missionary. In his enlightening discussion of how to witness effectively to Mormons, Dr. Rowe exhibits not only keen logic and detailed knowledge but an irenic spirit and gracious attitude. Here we have missionary apologetics at its best."

Vernon Grounds, chancellor, Denver Seminary

"Something is wrong with witness when one consistently wins arguments but never souls. The habits of the Mormon heart are not reshaped by confrontation with the gospel but by confession of the gospel. David Rowe teaches us lessons in faithful confession to Mormon culture. Live these lessons, and the lives of those around you will turn Godward."

Terry C. Muck, professor of mission and world religion,
Asbury Theological Seminary

"For over a century and a half, evangelicals have written books condemning Mormon belief and practice. Not surprisingly, these books engendered a style of evangelism focused on winning arguments, not people. Dave Rowe has written a new kind of book—one that endeavors to make the Good News actually *sound* like good news to Mormons. His three decades of ministry in Utah has given him insights into Mormon culture and the Mormon mind-set that are a tremendous help to those who want to reach their Mormon friends."

Ken Mulholland, founder and former president,
Salt Lake Theological Seminary

"What a fresh, creative approach to sharing the gospel with those of the Latter-day Saints faith! In his delightful narrative style, David encourages the reader to accompany him in his own journey in coming to understand how to relate to Mormons. He demonstrates a key understanding of Mormonism: it is not just another religion, another cult, but a culture. He does this without any compromise to the teachings of historic Christianity but displays a genuine love and respect for Mormons. From my own experience of pastoring a church in Utah for twenty years, I can't emphasize strongly enough that this is such an important concept to grasp if one is to be effective in relating to them. The questions at the end of each chapter are a great help toward applying these principles to our own situation."

Les Magee, former pastor of Washington Heights Church,
Salt Lake City

"I have been a serious student of the Mormon Church and Mormon culture for forty-five years. I grew up in the state of Utah, and I ministered as a pastor in Utah for thirty-three years. I have read dozens of books over the years about Mormon history; Mormon theology, beliefs, and practices; and how to witness to or share the gospel with Mormon people. This is the best book I have read on understanding Mormon culture and communicating effectively with Mormon people. David Rowe writes out of decades of experience of living in Utah and interacting with Mormon people. This is not a theoretical treatise, but rather a practical and compassionate approach to living constructively as a Protestant Christian in a setting dominated by Mormon culture."

Jeff Silliman, executive presbyter,
Presbytery of Riverside, San Bernardino, California

I MORMONS

I ♥ MORMONS

A New Way to
Share Christ with
Latter-day Saints

DAVID L. ROWE, PH.D.

BakerBooks
Grand Rapids, Michigan

Published by Baker Books
a division of Baker Publishing Group
P.O. Box 6287, Grand Rapids, MI 49516-6287
www.bakerbooks.com

Printed in the United States of America

Library of Congress Cataloging-in-Publication Data
Rowe, David L.
    I love Mormons : a new way to share Christ with Latter-day Saints /
David L. Rowe.
        p.   cm.
    Includes bibliographical references.
    ISBN 0-8010-6522-4 (pbk.)
    1. Missions to Mormoms. I. Title.
BV2627.R69 2005
266′.0088′2893—dc22   2005005245

Contents

Preface   9

Introduction   11

1 Hard-Won Lessons in Evangelistic Football: *A Personal Experience*   15

2 At the Heart of "The Forgotten Sector": *The Cultural Nerve Center*   23

3 Roots and Wings: *The Imprint of Mormon Culture*   37

4 Mormon Theology 101: *The Template of Official Beliefs*   53

5 101 Laboratory: *The So-Whats of Discussing Theology with Mormons*   67

6 Mormons in Transition: *The Travels and Travails*   85

7 Love It or Leave It: *Two Stories*   99

8 The Heart of the Matter: *Learning to Speak "Mormonese"*   113

9 Speaking Mormonese: *Stories and Sensibilities*   131

10 Concluding the Journey: *Is Your Church a Safe Harbor?*   147

   Appendix 1: The Articles of Faith of the Church of Jesus Christ of Latter-day Saints: *With Annotations by the Author*   161

   Appendix 2: Changes in Mormon Doctrine: *An Example*   165

   Appendix 3: Relating to Mormon Missionaries: *A Model Story*   169

   Notes   175

   A Selective Glossary of LDS Terms   179

   Resources   189

Preface

"We felt respected," said the Mormon student who lingered at the front of the lecture hall longer than all the other questioners. Five of her Latter-day Saints friends lingered with her, and all of them nodded their agreement. We were at Baylor University, and I had just given a long-planned, carefully crafted lecture titled "The Creed and Culture of Mormonism." The administrator who helped plan the event expected it to draw "twenty-two people, including you and me," but to everyone's astonishment, the three-hundred-seat hall was packed! The planners and I had prayed hard for precisely the above response from any Mormons who might attend. We were overjoyed.

Such respect for this people called Mormons, born of and carried on the wings of a deep love for them (despite deep disagreements with some of their distinctives), embodies the spirit as well as one of the major objectives of this book. My prayer, my dream, is that you, the reader, would come to understand Latter-day Saints and their culture and wed this understanding to a profound love and respect for them that they will sense as you relate to them. *This* is how bridges for the biblical gospel will be built into their world, their lives, and even their worldwide church.

This prayer, this dream, is not mine alone. And truth be told, it did not originate with me. I'm articulating an innovative approach crafted out of the collective reflection and hard-won experiences of my colleagues and me at Salt Lake Theological Seminary. We have sought to live well and love well for Christ as traditional Christians in the context of a Mormon culture. Our approach was distilled most definitively in 2000 with a series of training videos we developed called Bridges: Helping Mormons Discover God's Grace. This book follows the contours of that series and is designed in part to serve as a companion study to it. I quote freely—and enthusiastically—from the Bridges material.

So my first acknowledgment after the Lord Jesus Christ is to my seminary colleagues, especially founding president Ken Mulholland, who incarnate the concepts expressed here in their very lives and have helped me invaluably in providing resources and editing the manuscript. Thanks go as well to those willing to be interviewed for the book who have traveled roads I have not and so give life to what I write, especially Paul and Jenna Murphy, Dave and Jan Castro, Les Magee, and Scott McKinney. I'm also very grateful to Chad Allen, my editor at Baker, for encouraging me to write this book in the first place; he rightly saw the Bridges approach as a much-needed, new, and distinctive message on the subject of how traditional Christians can best relate to Mormons. It is a message whose time has come.

David Livingstone Rowe
October 1, 2004

Introduction

"The Happy Valley" they called it, back in 1975 when our family came to Salt Lake City, Utah. Some used the phrase with a certain admiration, maybe even a touch of hometown pride; others with a kind of smirking irony. Right away I picked up in the very tones of local parlance a sense of uneasy peace—this was a kind of geographic and cultural zone of unique beauty, yet bearing the atmosphere of a somewhat compromised "Zion." It was and remains a beautiful and rather curious place to live, a place nestled against the spectacular Wasatch Front of the Rocky Mountains and containing at city center a temple with a golden angel on top.

As traditional Christians, my family has learned to adapt to and even appreciate the physical and social ecology of this place, this curious new "Zion" settled by the pioneering people of the Church of Jesus Christ of Latter-day Saints (commonly called "Mormons" or simply "LDS"). Alongside other traditional Christians, we found ourselves on a quest to understand LDS people, their values, beliefs, and lifeways. We wanted to relate to them as Christ would have us relate. Though we non-Mormons had moved into the very capital of this worldwide movement, we desired to

learn how to touch Mormon lives everywhere with what
Christ had given us.

And learn we did, but not overnight. For many of us
outside the Mormon majority, it took years of cluelessness and pain, and I count myself as Exhibit A among
the many. Of the nearly thirty years my family and I have
lived and worked here, I suspect half of those years were
spent wandering in the desert of cluelessness (with its at-
tendant pain). My wife, Hazel, and I moved here just after
I graduated from seminary. Here we raised three children,
got involved in various ministries, and joined and have
been faithful to a church; here I finished a second master's
degree and a doctorate in communication. With many
fellow travelers in this unique terrain, especially my dear
colleagues at Salt Lake Theological Seminary, I've reflected
hard (both formally and in the "school of hard knocks") on
how best to communicate the Good News to LDS people.
This book is the result of that reflection.

Where We're Headed

You're about to take a journey in print that I hope will
help you forward on a journey of your own. We'll be looking first at contrasting types of experiences in relating to
LDS people (chapter 1). Then we'll explore the notion of
Mormon culture—the patterned behaviors, thoughts, and
values of LDS ethnicity—with a view to appreciating that
culture so we can relate with understanding (chapters 2
and 3). Next we'll examine in broad outline the theological
grid that forms one major piece of the culture's core; we will
endeavor in this exercise to make honest but nonbashing
comparison to traditional Christian doctrine and suggest
how best to discuss these issues with LDS people (chapters
4 and 5). Then we will move on to reflect on why and how
some journey out of Mormonism and some don't; we'll
also hear some sensitive, honest, and poignant stories of

LDS and former LDS people in transition, showing much in Mormon life they find attractive as well as some things they find disturbing or questionable (chapters 6 and 7). At the summit of the book is an exploration of the characteristically Mormon way of knowing about God and spiritual matters—and how we need to adapt our communication style to their way of knowing so the Good News can truly sound like good news (chapters 8 and 9). Finally, we'll look at some important moves traditional Christians and their churches can make to graciously welcome and support LDS people who visit or transition in, and then we'll draw overall conclusions (chapter 10). Incidentally, to respect and protect some of the persons quoted in these pages, I've used pseudonyms where appropriate.

Traveling through this book may be a personal enrichment project for you. As another option, use this book as a study guide for a group or class. Especially (though not exclusively) to facilitate this second option, you'll notice I've included questions and exercises at the end of each chapter in the section titled "For Discussion and More," and you may also find the material in the appendixes helpful for further probing. If you go with this option, which I strongly encourage, I hope these materials will enhance your journey through lively, light-producing discussions with fellow travelers. Now let the journey begin!

1

Hard-Won Lessons in Evangelistic Football

A Personal Experience

"The problem with the Bible bash," erupted my Mormon friend, "is that it just doesn't help people understand each other. Both sides—the Mormon and the non-Mormon—just keep raising their defenses, and often their voices, but no real listening goes on."

He was right, but I wouldn't figure that out enough to take it seriously for another fifteen years. Nevertheless, I had become acquainted enough with Mormon expressions to realize "Bible bash" was not a complimentary term. It meant he felt I was using the Bible to bash his faith and, more importantly, *him*.

Evangelistic Entry Pains

I was fresh on the scene in Salt Lake City, all optimistic, armed, and ready to engage. I figured I had the right artillery of arguments and verses, knew the Mormon system cold, and even understood the rules of engagement pretty well. And so I did. I had their religious system fairly mastered—on paper. Only slowly over the years would I come to learn that paper and systems are a lot easier to master than people; only slowly would I come to ask honestly, *should* I be trying to *master* Mormon people anyway?

I came to Salt Lake City on a mission as a Christian campus minister at the University of Utah in 1975. My colleagues in the ministry of which I was part dubbed me the "Mormon Slayer" and gave me the ironic title "Elder Rowe." I had taught seminars at conferences on the history and teachings of the LDS Church, and my colleagues were impressed with my grasp of both the Mormon system and the biblical response to it. I even knew how to quote and urge upon my hearers the Bible's verses about being loving and gracious in our witness to Mormons.

So here I was "engaged" in conversation with Jason, let's call him. And I'd just warmed up to the parry-and-thrust of some of my finest arguments—uh, graciously, of course—to get him to doubt Mormonism and trust the Bible and its Christ. It was so natural to me now, this set of combative reflexes, I didn't even think of it as arguing! We were simply having a discussion, weren't we? So when Jason called what we were doing a "Bible bash," I was immediately taken aback.

No, that's putting it too mildly: truth be told, I felt something stab at me, a nagging something that told me this "discussion" was over. It had become yet another chagrined charade, a missing of the point, a disconnect, a terminal impasse—in short, a painful failure in the relationship. He had just shut down and, what's more, had shut *us* down.

A Traditional Way: The Doctrinal "Warrior Saint"

By now I was getting familiar with this pattern of contact, "discussion," recoil, and shutdown, having been at it for about three years. And by this point, that stabbing feeling I got, joined like a Siamese twin to a feeling of despair, had started to intensify beyond what I considered tolerable. Frankly, though, I just *did not know* what else to do but shake it off, suit up with my spiritual armor, and ready myself for yet another spin at the same jousting game.

So, like most other Utah ministers with whom I compared notes, I took some refuge in putting the best face on it while proceeding full steam ahead, staying the course, making another charge. The best face we put on turned out to be some form of makeover that left us traditional Christian "warrior saints" looking pretty noble at the end of the day. After all, we were just faithfully and honestly "preaching the truth," right? We were simply called to proclaim the gospel and leave the results to God, amen? We were powerless to keep our Mormon friends from thinking we were somehow attacking *them* instead of their doctrine, weren't we? (Uh, by the way, we *were* their friends, right?) We couldn't help it if "the god of this world has blinded the minds of unbelievers" (2 Cor. 4:4), could we? Ours was not to reason why but simply to keep on keeping on and suffering those battle wounds for the Lord. Wasn't all this the plain and simple truth of the matter?

Well, a lot was plain and simple back then, but not much of it was truthful. That one could enjoy friendship with Mormons and enjoy the title "Mormon Slayer" at the same time was patently disingenuous. Proceeding as if one could "Bible bash" without raising defenses and coming across as attacking amounted to gross silliness as well as flat-out cluelessness about human communication. Acting like we who evangelized by trafficking in "what's wrong with Mormonism" and "evidence against Mormonism" were really "just preaching the truth" or "simply proclaiming the

gospel" bordered on self-congratulatory delusionalism. To
believe our proclamation style truly created no offense but
"the offense of the cross" was an offense to the truth! Even
if many we met were "blinded" by "the god of this world,"
it now seems to me that in order to help them we had to
deal with a blindness of our own, a peculiar blindness to
the sinewy, pulsating, dust-and-dreams, soulful reality of
the Mormon people as first and most of all *people*.

In those days I was just not ready to recognize, let alone
deal with, the blindness in my home court—what Jesus
would call "the beam" in my own eye, which was steadily
growing from telephone pole to sequoia proportions. I was
not ready to face its implications. Why did I do this confrontational, warrior-mode evangelism with LDS people?
Yes, for one thing it was all I knew, all I'd seen by way of
modeling, and the way I'd been trained by both formal and
informal mentors. But it seems to me there was something
else lurking in the depths and driving this approach, something we traditional Christians didn't like to think about,
something called fear. Mormons and other religious groups
threaten us, in part simply because they are "other" and
perhaps odd—"not us." I'm not sure why this should scare
us, but sometimes it does. We revert to fight-or-flight reflexes, quite unlike Jesus, who was secure in the love of the
Father for all people so that he was able to embrace with
uncanny comfort the whole range of humanity, including
Romans, Samaritans, Pharisees, prostitutes, and lepers.
We would do well to cultivate that kind of security in the
love of God for all people.

And I'm convinced there's another part of our fear that
runs deeper: religions like Mormonism, rooted heavily
(though only partially) in New England Protestant Christianity, may stand as an indictment to Protestants because
they arose to compensate for some perceived failure in that
Christian movement. The founder of Mormonism, Joseph
Smith Jr., saw disunity among the Christian denominations
and started a single "true Church" that he believed would

unify all members and spell an end to denominational schism; he saw traditional churches not always caring for the poor and needy, so he started a church with its own welfare system. I've often felt that part of our own blindness amounts to fear of the reminder of our own failures, a reminder that stands up in front of us in the form of the other group's compensations. So rather than confess and fight the fear within us, we too often would rather go on the attack against their aberrant doctrines!

We simply need to do what I was not ready to do back then. We need to confess, then overcome our fears and blindness by God's grace and find a better way to touch our LDS friends with the love of God out of our own security in that love.

Another Way: Touchdowns for Jesus

Let's see if a second snapshot from Utah culture can paint the picture of a redemptive alternative to the Bible bash. Scott, a friend of mine who pastors a steadily growing evangelical church in the vicinity of Brigham Young University, loves sports. As a hobby and a way of engaging the lives of his neighbors (mostly Mormon folk, of course), he coaches Little League football or other sports teams every year. He's coached Little League baseball, soccer, girls' softball, flag football, and high school football. As he reported to me and as others confirmed, in the course of time, parents began clamoring to get their sons or daughters on Scott's team, not necessarily because his was often a winning team but mainly because of the coaching style they'd heard about and wanted their children to experience.

What they'd heard is that Scott carries a seriously exuberant, positively reinforcing, genuinely caring style that simply stands in stark contrast to what a lot of other coaches in the league exhibit. "This is a *tremendously* competitive culture, and it's *all* about winning at any cost," said a friend who has observed Scott's coaching. The expectations to excel run stratospherically high, and for the sake of those expectations, parents put "unbelievable pressures" on the kids. Coaches do the same and simply compound the pressures.

To put a finer point on this analysis, let me revisit an experience I had when my grade-school-aged daughter joined a girls' soccer team. One brisk morning as I watched the practice, I heard their coach berate the girls rather mercilessly for losing the last game. Among his comments were memorable words something like the following: "Listen! On Sunday morning when you go to Sunday school, you learn you're supposed to 'love your neighbor' and all that stuff. That's fine for Sunday morning, but this is Saturday. When you come here, forget that Sunday school stuff! This is where you gotta learn to crush, maim, and destroy those girls on the other team!" This memory of my daughter's foray into Utah "sportsmanship" certainly resonated with the description I was hearing of typical Little League football experience.

But Scott proved different. His presence and his actions displayed a love of the game and a love for the kids, neither love compromising the other, and it became clear that he respected them—and their parents—in a way that was distinctive for the sake of Christ. Berating didn't happen on his team, but lots of fun and encouragement and good sportsmanship did, not to mention prayer and a remarkable number of wins!

Now comes the rub. Scott remembers one family in particular that was directly impacted in the span of a few seasons: all members of the family ended up leaving the LDS Church and being baptized into his church, and later another whole family of their relatives were likewise baptized. A leader in the congregation told me that he recalls five entire families of former Mormons being baptized into their church during those few seasons. Scott adds, "The number of contacts that were made and the number of people that still visit our church from the community because of that involvement is still being felt. The impact that this has had is more than the direct impact on families. It has said to the community—and to members of our own church—that we are here to make a contribution to the community."

In large part, all this is simply due to the faithful, sensitive witness of Coach Scott. Did Scott evangelize the families with his arsenal of arguments and confrontational evidence against Mormonism? No, not one bit. Instead they experienced something good on the personal level. It seems the parents just plain got more and more curious about what kind of faith produced folks of such truly Christlike character as they saw in their kids' coach. So they pursued more and more of what they had first tasted and loved in their experience with the football team. They started hanging around Scott and his friends, then visited the church to taste the vibrant worship, then asked more and more questions, then received the gift of salvation in Christ and became active in the congregation. Impressive attitudes eclipsed impressive arguments. Incarnation eclipsed information.

Getting Beyond the "Bible Bash"

Perhaps you resonate with some of the experiences above as your life has intersected with the lives of Mormon friends, neighbors, co-workers, or even relatives. Maybe, like me, you've done your fair share of bumbling and offending and learned some hard-won lessons. Maybe you've sensed something is wrong with the Bible bash, so you've chosen to keep your distance from Mormons—to "live and let live"—yet you know something's wrong with this approach too. And maybe you have, or wish you had, the gift of a "Scott" somewhere in your life to inspire you and point to a better way.

You may not live in Salt Lake City or one of the other cities of the intermountain West where LDS settlers have formed the culture and still form the majority. The cultural stamp or ethos of Mormonism nevertheless will have left its imprint on the Mormon people God has put in your life. And if we traditional Christians sincerely wish to get beyond the stalemating pattern of the Bible bash or the avoidance implied by "live and let live," if we really wish to particularize for LDS people Paul's exhortation to "become all things to all men . . . for the sake of the gospel" (1 Cor. 9:22–23), we must begin by taking that cultural imprint seriously.

For Discussion and More

1. Relive one or two experiences you've had with Mormon friends or relatives by retelling your story. You could do this in a group, class, or private journal.
2. Now looking carefully at what you've just relived and retold, see if you can gather lessons from it about how you were taught to relate to LDS people, strengths and weaknesses of what you did, and how your LDS friends or relatives responded.
3. Respond to the positive model of Scott in this chapter, commenting on what went right and why. Is there a downside to this approach? Do you have a "Scott" you've observed? If so, tell about what you've noticed and would like to emulate.
4. Discuss how the Bible *should* be used with Mormon people, if not in a "bash."
5. Consider recording interviews with three to five LDS people on a cassette or notepad. Ask each simply to give their impressions of traditional Christians and tell how they feel these Christians relate to them. If you're in a group or class, share the responses.

2

At the Heart of "The Forgotten Sector"

The Cultural Nerve Center

Let's begin with a short quiz.

How do you suppose you would answer the following question: what ward do you belong to? It is a common question here in Salt Lake City, and we non-Mormon locals sometimes think we could have answered it more easily, perhaps, if we'd been in the waiting room of a hospital.

If you are a nineteen-year-old male (or female, though to a much lesser degree), what rite of passage are you expected to fulfill?

In terms of its meaning and power to your people, what modern historical event ranks equal in importance to the crucifixion of Christ?

All the above items point to a particular example of an experienced, ubiquitous reality among humans called "culture." A major and foundational claim I am making right up front is that *the Mormon movement is a culture.* Certainly at its core is a religion, institutionalized as the Church of Jesus Christ of Latter-day Saints, and certainly that religious system serves as the wellspring of virtually all else in the culture, but the culture is much, much more than just the standard beliefs and practices of the system.

In this chapter, I'll be focusing on the culture as manifest in Utah, the nerve center of worldwide Mormonism, to give us a sense of the basic pattern that has spread all over the world from this center. Knowing the details of this culture is valuable, but a caveat is certainly in order: though many elements of the basic cultural pattern (e.g., abstinence from coffee, tea, and alcoholic drinks) are universally present wherever the Mormon Church has gone, some cultural elements (e.g., foods, local folk dances, and some optional church meetings) vary as the Church adapts to local environments. Nevertheless, from the almost Guinness-sized rate of ice cream consumption in this "Mormon Zion" to the closing down of adult theaters and porn shops to the fireworks display on July 24 (which outstrips the one on July 4), there flourishes here a set of practices, beliefs, and values that go far beyond—though they're not disconnected from—the basic religious dogma and framework.

Culture 101

Just what do we mean by the term *culture?* Consider four definitions:

1. The total pattern of human life in society, including four aspects—a mental road map, the sum total of our lived experience, a system of values that directs our activities, and a way to define the limits of possibility (Thom Hopler).[1]
2. A way of thinking, feeling, and believing; the group's knowledge stored up for future use—a set of standardized orientations to recurrent problems (Clyde Kluckhohn).[2]

3. The collective, symbolic discourse of a community on knowledge, beliefs, and values (Talcott Parsons).[3]
4. The patterned way in which people do things together—more specifically, an integrated system of beliefs (about God or reality or ultimate meaning), of values (about what is true, good, beautiful, and normative), of customs (how to behave, relate to others, talk, pray, dress, work, play, trade, farm, eat, etc.), and of institutions that express these beliefs, values, and customs (government, law courts, temples or churches, family, schools, hospitals, factories, shops, unions, clubs, etc.), that binds a society together and gives it a sense of identity, dignity, security, and continuity (The Willowbank Report).[4]

Notice with me some common elements in the definitions. One is a sense of *pattern*. Culture is not random but orderly; it occurs in sets of patterns (e.g., manners repeated the same way over and over; red lights hanging over an intersection always mean stop; in a line of strangers at the theater or bank, you must always join at the back).

Second, culture is *social*. It occurs in groups of people, usually known as ethnic groups, who agree together to perpetuate these patterns among themselves. That agreement, of course, does not usually come about by vote or other formal process, but rather it gets learned and affirmed and passed on more subtly and slowly, sometimes even implicitly, "from our mother's knee." After we watch Daddy drive, park, and buy things for several years, and after a few dozen "Billy-we-don't-throw-food-at-the-table" or "Did-you-say-'please'?" exhortations, we know how to comply with the norms our group has decided constitute proper behavior. This implicit, second-nature, stored-up knowledge becomes a "mental road map" to guide our behavior in all the specific situations of life we typically face. Our entire people group shares the same road map.

Third, the basic aspects of culture seem invariably to include, in some form, *beliefs*, *values*, and *behaviors* (or *customs*). Personally, I like to sum up these aspects under two general headings, *worldviews* and *lifeways*. The former heading includes the understandings of the group about what is real and what is valuable, and the latter includes the normal and customary practices or living patterns of the group (rituals, institutional protocols, manners, and so on). These patterns, I might add, get communicated in highly symbolic terms—handshakes, kisses, appropriate attire, the meaning of punctuality, the use of titles, and the positions and arrival times of cars at a four-way stop. All of these and others are symbols we come to understand and retrieve from our learned storehouse, that is, "the group's knowledge stored up for future use."

Fourth, please, please don't fail to notice with me one more crucial matter about culture: as the Willowbank Report's definition puts it, culture gives the people group "a sense of *identity*, *dignity*, *security*, and *continuity*" (emphasis mine). Being connected to my culture, then, becomes a "home court" in which I know who I am (identity). For example, as a white, Protestant American I tend to be optimistic (things will ultimately turn out for the good, and the wolf will stay away from *our* door), somewhat industrious (having been trained in the lifeways of the famed "Protestant work ethic"), and rather individualistic (social institutions, including the church, exist for my good, not vice versa). In my cultural home court, I also grow in my sense of importance or esteem (dignity)—everything from a simple but honorific greeting ritual (handshake, bow, or kiss) to a parent's smile of delight, a coach's "well done," or the conferring of a diploma serves to tell me in the language of cultural symbol that I'm important. And my particular world of cultural symbol is the zone in which I feel safe, or perhaps competent or streetwise (security). Whether I'm buying a movie ticket or applying for a job or praying in church, I know the ropes, know how things get done, and generally feel unthreatened, because I'm among people I can trust to have a common understanding of those ropes. It is this world of home-court symbols, then—how to do romantic courting, behave in a restaurant, buy and sell, worship, and on and on—that we pass on to our children and grandchildren (continuity). All of these become an intergenerational glue for our ethnic group.

What? These Ordinary Americans, an *Ethnic Group*?

This matter of ethnicity returns us to our main point: the Mormon community, make no mistake, is a unique ethnic group with its own culture.

For many of us who have logged some years in Utah, we didn't really "get it" at first. What we didn't get was that this place looks and sounds much the same as any other place in the United States, but it isn't. Slowly something began to dawn on us: the social ecology; the morals of most of the people around us; the built environment of houses, churches, and city settlements; the political and business climate; and numerous other factors made us aware that this area and its occupants form a distinct and unusual pocket in the country quite unlike any other. So virtually unnoticeable is it that missions scholars and leaders have dubbed this pocket of the American continent "The Forgotten Sector," because historically it has been the least evangelized and has the least infrastructure of traditional Christianity in the nation. As we outsiders ("Gentiles," in Utah parlance) began to realize, perhaps the words "This is the place" did not mean it is the place for *us*.

In a certain historic sense, we were right. Those famous words, attributed to Brigham Young on July 24, 1847, signified when they were spoken a sense of isolation for the community he led. What he meant was, "This is *our* place," implying a decisive boundary between "us" and "them"—to put it more plainly, between "us Mormons" and the inhabitants of the United States. At the time, you may recall, the Great Basin desert area, which included the land that became Salt Lake City, and the geography north and south of it were all part of the territory *outside* the United States and its government. Young, a great leader and masterful colonizer, brought his people here to escape "them" so his community could live and prosper in peace.

We need to see there were good and understandable reasons the Mormon people felt the need to isolate themselves and form their own distinctive society. Quite distinctive it was, and to a remarkable extent continues to be. So sooner or later it dawns on us who moved here innocently unaware of this distinctiveness (like parachuters dropped into some very unfamiliar, foreign zone) that the people who settled this place and continue to dominate it truly have a *culture* all their own! Now, by no means am I suggesting we were completely ignorant or unaware of everything about the Mormon people. As the previous chapter makes plain, a lot of us knew the belief system cold (at least the textbook version) well before coming here. Some of us knew beliefs of the LDS from A to Z! But a belief system is only one slice of the whole pie, only one component of a whole culture holding a people group together. Besides, not all the local "believers" even believe the belief system! This we did not "get."

We did not "get" and so did not prepare to take seriously this notion of ethnicity. Of course some of us who studied our Great Commission theology with a bit of precision may have realized Jesus used the word *ethne*, the root of "ethnic," when he commanded us to "make disciples of all *nations*" (Matt. 28:19). Yes, our Lord was telling us to "make disciples of all *ethnic groups*," but we did not think of the Mormons this way. Somehow Chinese people groups qualified, as did the Berbers of Morocco, the Sawi of New Guinea, the Jewish in Tel Aviv, the Hutu in Rwanda, and even the various Native American tribes of this continent—but not the Mormons. We did not primarily think of them as one of the *ethne*, or people groups, at the heart of Jesus' command. We thought of them in terms of orthodoxy and not in terms of ethnicity, depreciated their aberrant beliefs, and did not appreciate their colorful lifeways. We reduced their movement to a cult and did not recognize it as a culture. We thought theologically, not missiologically; we put on our countercult hats when we should have put on our missionary hats.

As a small example of this ongoing, evangelical Christian bias to reduce Mormonism to a "cult," you need look no further than the category name above the bar code on the back of this book. It reads "Cults," you notice. I'll tell you why. Publishers who market to Christian booksellers must give a book the conventional category used by those booksellers so the book will end up shelved in stores alongside other books of the same kind—in this case, books on reaching out to Mormons. As an author, I have no control over this practice and the institutional bias that drives it. I'm arguing it's high time we rethink this bias.

One resource some of us at Salt Lake Theological Seminary bumped into helped us make the paradigm shift. Reflecting on ethnicity and the call of Jesus to evangelize the *ethne*, we found to our wondering eyes a full chapter on Mormons in (of all places) *The Harvard Encyclopedia of American Ethnic Groups*! The scholars who edited this unusual encyclopedia define in its opening chapter what they mean by an ethnic group, claiming such a group is typically characterized by some sixteen trademarks or at least a large number of them. Among these characteristics the editors list a common language, a body of folklore, a particular history, migration patterns, marriage practices, and a sense of boundary to separate "us" from "them." Unblushingly, unhesitatingly, and without qualification, the author of the chapter on Mormons, the late Dr. Dean May of the Department of History at the University of Utah, chronicles the LDS story and draws out their characteristics as an ethnic group. Some time later I met and initiated a personal relationship with Dr. May, who described himself to me as "a believing Mormon."

What comes out in May's treatment? The kind of, and sheer amount of, information he includes makes one wonder how we ever could have *missed* this notion of Mormons as an ethnic group! Some of the items mentioned above give us part of May's picture. Most obviously, the religion of the LDS Church shows itself uniquely North American as a cultural derivative from New England Christendom. The Mormon people have as the launchpad for this religion a founding story—Joseph Smith's "first vision"—with a continuing legendry developing afterward (not to imply that these are fictional tales, but certainly many are heroic tales). The Mormons have in their history both a powerful sequence of migration patterns and a marriage practice that is very distinctive in the Western world (i.e., polygamy). They also have been shaped greatly by the above-mentioned sense of isolation in their early history of settling here in the intermountain West, reinforcing the "us-them" boundary. These and a good number of other distinctives more than adequately establish Mormons as an ethnic group—a people group with their own worldview and lifeways, that is, their own unique culture.

Let me flesh this out a bit by inviting you to notice some of the textural details of this unusual culture. Consider the following examples, drawn from information available at the Utah Travel Council in Salt Lake City (only a small sampling of the entire inventory, I assure you):

- Temple Square, the biggest tourist attraction in Salt Lake City, not only serves as the symbolic center of the LDS Church (its equivalent of the Vatican or the worship center in Mecca) but also sits at the center of the city street system. Geographically, the language of visual symbol is articulated as a grid of numbered streets that radiate outward in the four directions of the compass from "00, 0," which is Temple Square. Going south, for example, the east-west running streets are labeled "South Temple," "1st South," "2nd South," "3rd South," and so on, and this pattern happens in every direction. All goes back to the focal point, the temple. You'll see this geographic imprint, by the way, wherever LDS people have been the majority in founding a town—not just in Utah.

- The largest private employer in the state of Utah is Brigham Young University. This school, owned by the LDS Church, boasts a very fine reputation with a clean, well-enforced moral climate (no alcohol or tobacco on campus) and a traditionally excellent football team. Unlike many colleges and universities in America that were founded as Christian schools but are now secularized, BYU has remained truly anchored to its Mormon roots and commitments.

- Business and technological enterprises seem to be attracted to the Utah market as well, bearing testimony to the characteristic industry and organizational genius of Mormon culture. In the final decade of the twentieth century, Utah was considered one of the nation's "high-tech hot spots," due to which, in large part, the state's household income skyrocketed in the national ratings from twenty-ninth to eighth.

- Salt Lake City is the genealogy capital of the world. This will come as no surprise to those aware of the culture and the Mormon Church's teachings on baptism for dead people who await salvation. The world's largest collection of genealogical information exists here in the LDS Family History Library—well over 2,000,000,000 names, 711,000 microfiche, and 278,000 books. Connected to this library is a system of 3,400 satellite libraries in 65 countries.

- The Mormon Tabernacle Choir, 320 voices strong, has deservedly achieved the label "Choir of the Presidents," having sung for every U.S. president since William Howard Taft. Started only one month after the Mormon pioneers reached Salt Lake Valley, the choir certainly displays an intergenerational commitment to the value of religious music (and more) at the center of LDS community life. The choir's program *Music and the Spoken Word*, broadcast twice weekly over 1,500 radio and television stations, is the longest-running network radio program in the world. Also, the choir has released over 150 albums, 5 of which are gold and 2 platinum. This group is a universal icon for Mormons.

- The Latter-day Saint Humanitarian Center gives assistance to those in need in amounts valued at tens of millions of dollars annually. The center has reached people in 147 different countries with its programs and projects to give away food, medical equipment, clothing, and educational supplies.

Besides statistics and demographic data such as the above, this sense of culture in relation to Mormon people crops up in literature. Stephen White's murder-mystery novel *Higher Authority*, set in Salt Lake City, contains several passages rich in their depictions of Mormon culture. Some come through the eyes of outsiders, some through the eyes of insiders. Listen to a few comments by one of his characters, an outsider.

Salt Lake City isn't just a funny western town that used to be full of polygamists and now has a great choir and wants to host the Winter Olympics. This . . . is the center of one of the fastest-growing and wealthiest Christian churches in the world. Salt Lake City is a true religious capital—a major one, like Rome, or Jerusalem, or Tehran. . . .

It's hard to explain the culture here, and I don't know if I'm doing a good job. I'm afraid you actually have to live here to understand it. . . . Some of the time living here feels normal. It's a beautiful, peaceful place—clean, not too much crime, wonderful mountains, great climate. Then one day I realized that it's the most segregated place I've ever lived. There are two absolutely parallel communities here: one LDS, one gentile. . . . I have no close friends who are LDS—none. And none of my friends have friends who are LDS. . . . I don't want this to sound anti-Mormon. It's easy to make fun of the Mormons. People have been doing it, apparently, from the start. See, with one another, these saints can be remarkable people. They help each other as unselfishly as you could imagine. . . . As a group of people they are absolutely consumed with the welfare of their own community. . . . What they do is they entice you with the sense of community.[5]

Mormon Social Glue: Five Core Values

The descriptions, facts, and statistics you have just read give a little of the texture of what life is like for this ethnic group. If we pull our lens back a bit from the trees to a focal point on the forest, we may see some major aspects of the pattern coming together. Here are five core values of Mormon community:

1. *A solid work ethic*. LDS folk become from childhood very responsible, entrepreneurial, industrious people. They seize opportunities and do not fear hard work, both in Church life and in the marketplace. It is no accident that Salt Lake City has remained one of the country's most attractive climates for business and technology over the last quarter century.
2. *Economic conservatism*. The gaining and maintaining of fairly large investments and sums of wealth marks this community. You can find here a good number of prominent citizens who own large businesses. Larry Miller, who owns auto dealerships as well as the Utah Jazz basketball team, and the Marriott family, who

own the famous hotel chain, are faithful Mormon folk. On a more middle-class level as well, people learn to hold stable jobs and save for goals like a college education or a two-year mission.

3. *A strong emphasis on the family.* "Families Are Forever" plaques appear on hundreds of living-room walls in Utah, announcing a core belief. The traditional family gets affirmed and celebrated here; newer "alternative families" (like homosexual parents with children) do not. The family is the basic unit of LDS Church life, with the structured, once-a-week Family Home Evening program and other initiatives to strengthen the unity of the family. In Mormon culture, "family" is about as close as one can get to a cultural "god word" (a core term in a culture, signifying an ultimate value).

4. *A strong emphasis on clean and healthy living.* This is definitely *not* the place for cigarette sales, not too much better for liquor, and as a character in *Higher Authority* says, "It's hard to find a good cup of coffee around here." Right in the LDS scriptures, the faithful read a divine command forbidding the use of such ı armful substances. Laws and social institutions reflect this: in Utah, for example, alcoholic substances (except 3.2 percent beer) cannot be sold in the grocery stores, only in state-owned liquor stores, so alcohol becomes highly regulated. We who live here have also watched as adult theaters and porn shops tried to make it in town after town and had their doors closed again and again.

5. *Cooperation.* Mormon people are nothing if not organized. They constantly pull together for events or activities, having refined the art of communal cooperation to nearly professional expertise. They have been a "help-one-another" people from the beginning, when they had to carve out their niche in this desert by building homes, farms, and temples together and fighting

the elements and common enemies to establish themselves. They worked communally even in their trading practices: the main shopping center in Salt Lake City, encouraging people to support each other, was titled Zion's *Cooperative* Mercantile Institution. The earliest symbol of the state was its name *Deseret*, drawn from the Book of Mormon and meaning "honeybee." Utah is still known as the Beehive State, an image on which one could hardly improve for the industry and cooperation of these remarkable people.

"Forgotten" but Not Gone

This area may be the Forgotten Sector for historic mission efforts by traditional Christians, but its people have far from gone away and disappeared! Among other things, the successful hosting of the 2002 Winter Olympics sealed the position of Salt Lake City on the world map. The Mormon people—and their culture—must be better understood to be better reached. We will turn in the next chapter to their fascinating history as a people.

For Discussion and More

1. Can you describe the term *culture* in your own words? Try it, and then add some examples of aspects of a culture you're familiar with, whether your own or another.
2. Name some historical and social factors that led to the geographic corridor with Utah in its center being labeled "The Forgotten Sector." To what extent are those factors still valid today?
3. Why do you suppose traditional, biblical Christians have not primarily thought and acted in terms that seriously recognized Mormonism as a culture?

4. Describe at least three core values of Mormon culture; then evaluate each of the three in light of historic, biblical Christian understanding.

5. See if you can discern some universals of Mormon culture (values, beliefs, and lifeways you'd see anywhere, not just in Salt Lake City) that are positive or at least neutral in the light of biblical faith. Discuss how understanding these can help us build bridges of communication into the lives of LDS people.

3

Roots and Wings

The Imprint of Mormon Culture

A classmate from outside Utah whom I'd met while doing graduate studies at the University of Utah surprised me one day in the middle of a conversation. I'd asked him if he was a Mormon, to which he replied with an oddly dismissive grin, "I'm a *cultural* Mormon." At the time I was not sure I knew what that meant. Today I know.

A signature set of values, beliefs, and lifeways tends to mark LDS community wherever we find it. From Sydney to Salt Lake City, from Utah to Uganda, among all varieties from "believing Mormons" to "cultural Mormons," we can observe the trademarks of what holds them all together—the glue called culture. Of course some variations occur from place to place as the core of this glue is adapted to local traditions and practices, yet that core is remarkably universal: Mormons in Holland, I recently learned, hold church services on Christmas day (like traditional Dutch Christians, unlike Mormons in the United States), but neither there nor here nor anywhere on the globe will they be found drinking coffee, tea, or alcohol at their gatherings. Having introduced and defined that universal glue in the previous chapter, we want to look at the roots and wings of it here—where it comes from and how it "flies" in the real world.

Legacy and Legacy

The LDS promotional film *Legacy* makes a good starting place for our foray into the roots of Mormon culture. In various venues of the LDS Church, such as historic sites and tourist centers around the world, this film or films like it feature something of the story of the LDS Church's history and faith. Embedded in that history, we viewers see the filmmaker's version of the celebrated values, vision, and virtues of the Mormon legacy. Endearingly and with top-drawer production techniques, *Legacy* shows Eliza, a wise and gentle Mormon lady of advanced years, with her granddaughter on her lap, recounting to the child her memories of the early days of "our people."

Those early days go all the way back to some of the first movements and gatherings under the leadership of Joseph Smith Jr., whom all Mormons recognize as the founding prophet of their religion. Woven around the personal story of a charming romance between the grandmother in her marriageable youth and her suitor from England, we have the Mormon community's story. Settling in two Missouri locations as the new church begins to grow at an astronomical rate during the early 1830s, the Saints begin experiencing persecution at the hands of cruel neighbors and must repeatedly leave homes behind to flee for safety. Missourians are pictured as opposing and violently attacking the Mormons simply because the LDS are "against slavery" and "will elect a Mormon sheriff." The Saints persevere through this and move on to build a temple and a riverbank town in Nauvoo, Illinois, but they suffer their prophet's

death by angry mob action. Finally, they heroically cross
the plains under their new leader, Brigham Young, to settle
in the Great Basin, with Salt Lake City becoming their hub
and headquarters for all future expansions.

What understanding can we gain through such promotional accounts as *Legacy*? We understand what is valorized and celebrated in Mormon culture by noticing how
Mormons present their story to the world (and to insiders).
So, the big picture here (so to speak) portrays a persever-
ing but persecuted people of great faith and industry—a
story of overcoming odds and adversaries in the die-hard
pursuit of a distinctive vision. We can note the following
about the film:

- A heartwarming glow of candlelit sepia tones pervades
  the style, showing values of nostalgia and tender personal emotion.
- Pure, kind, innocent, visionary leaders remain basically unflawed. (Smith, for example, comes off as a
  child-hugging, soft-spoken man with great wisdom.)
- Persecution against Mormons by their neighbors,
  always unprovoked and quite violent, is taken as a
  badge of the Mormons' authenticity as divinely chosen people; Smith even states in a public speech in
  Nauvoo, "I should be like a fish out of water if I were
  out of persecution."
- Very conventional courtship and marriage practices
  reinforce strong commitment to the traditional nu-
  clear family. (Note: Not even a hint of polygamy appears in this film, though it was practiced at that time,
  and ironically Eliza herself, according to historians,
  was a plural wife of Joseph Smith!)
- Community solidarity shows a great help-one-another
  ethos.
- Hard work and industry is portrayed in the building
  of temples and whole cities.

- Perseverance through thick and thin is shown as the pioneers display a rugged, never-give-up heroism in crossing the plains at great sacrifice and then building a major "new Zion" in the desert.
- The Mormons have great faith in God's providence and special care to protect them and sustain them.

All in all, *Legacy* does indeed give us a tradition-rich image of the historical identity of the Mormon people—even though careful historians find it more than a little "sanitized." Persecuted, religious, industrious, communal, and sacrificial as their forebears truly were, Mormons take pride in passing on such narratives to their children and grandchildren.

Hingepoints and Imprints: A Closer Look at the Story

As the epic of the Mormons' travels and travails gets passed down through the generations, its major lessons about "why we are who we are" get passed on as well. This story with its powerful legacy has made an indelible, deep imprint on the cultural "we" of Mormon community. We can understand this legacy more fully, more definitively, by focusing on seven hingepoints of Mormon history and how they have imprinted the social psyche of this ethnic group. If we sincerely and seriously want to know our Mormon friends so we can communicate with them, especially on sensitive matters of faith, we must understand these seven major lessons.

1. The First Vision of Joseph Smith (1820)

At the age of only fourteen, Joseph Smith Jr. of Palmyra, New York, claimed he had had a vision. His followers right up to the present have believed it was an earthshaking, world-changing vision that inaugurated "the latter days" and gave them the foundational belief at the core of who they are.

Amid what LDS historians report as a time of great re-
vival in the various churches of upstate New York, Smith
got confused about which church (or denomination) to
join. So he decided to ask God to make good on his words
in James 1:5, which read (in the King James Version he
had), "If any of you lack wisdom, let him ask of God, that
giveth to all men liberally, and upbraideth not; and it shall
be given him." He prayed in the woods near his home, now
famously known to LDS people as "the sacred grove," and
after an immediate assault by a dark power and a hair-
raising struggle for deliverance, he reportedly received
this answer:

> I saw a pillar of light exactly over my head, above the bright-
> ness of the sun, which descended gradually until it fell upon
> me. It no sooner appeared than I found myself delivered
> from the enemy which held me bound. When the light
> rested upon me I saw two Personages, whose brightness
> and glory defy all description, standing above me in the
> air. One of them spake unto me, calling me by name and
> said, pointing to the other—*"This is My Beloved Son. Hear
> Him!"*
>
> My object in going to inquire of the Lord was to know
> which of all the sects was right, that I might know which
> to join. No sooner, therefore, did I get possession of myself,
> so as to be able to speak, than I asked the Personages who
> stood above me in the light, which of all the sects was right
> (for at this time it had never entered into my heart that all
> were wrong)—and which I should join. I was answered
> that I must join none of them, for they were all wrong; and
> the Personage who addressed me said that all their creeds
> were an abomination in his sight; that those professors
> were all corrupt; that: *"they draw near to me with their lips,
> but their hearts are far from me, they teach for doctrines the
> commandments of men, having a form of godliness, but they
> deny the power theoreof."* He again forbade me to join with
> any of them; and many other things did he say unto me,
> which I cannot write at this time. When I came to myself
> again, I found myself lying on my back, looking up into

heaven. When the light had departed, I had no strength; but soon recovering in some degree, I went home.[1]

This text as it functions in the LDS community is what culture analysts would call a *founding story*. Mormons receive it and regard it with the same awe with which Jewish people regard the story of Moses and the burning bush or Buddhists regard the story of Gautama attaining his moment of "enlightenment" beneath the tree. Let's notice some specifics about Smith's account.

First, it's religious. Unlike a pot-of-gold dream about business and wealth or a Constantine-like vision about military conquest and empire, this is about God and church. It specifies that God the Father is a "Personage" with a human body (more on this in the next chapter) and, furthermore, no institutional church has his approval since "they were all wrong" and "an abomination in his sight."

Second, it's exclusive. Smith was to join none of the sects and would eventually be led to start his own, which would become the exclusively right church, the "one true church" of Jesus Christ on the face of the earth.

Third, it's Christianesque. Linked to statements and images from the Bible—James 1:5, the Transfiguration-like visitation bathed in light and using the "My Beloved Son" statement, and the quote from Jesus about the "form of godliness"—the account gets wrapped in the form of biblical faith. The rhetoric works to convey the message, "If you believe the Bible, you should believe this vision."

And of course the LDS faithful do, thus becoming imprinted by the cornerstone belief of their worldview and value system. The First Vision establishes for them an undying, unquestioning belief in their succession of modern prophets, Smith being the first. Still today a standard, almost creedal statement of testimony heard again and again in their meetings is, "I believe Joseph Smith was a prophet of God." Smith's successor prophets carry the same weight, so often the current one is named, but the overriding imprint is the often-repeated statement, "The heavens are open," implying the LDS prophet is the only way God can and does keep his communication current with us humans.

This imprint on the core of the Mormon mind-set also includes the convictions that Jesus and the Father are two separate "Gods" (because that's what Joseph saw), that the church is essentially an institution, that only the LDS institution belongs to Jesus Christ, and that this all flows inevitably as the next step of God's revelation after the Bible.

2. The Early Persecutions (ca. 1838)

A series of struggles characterizes Mormon history and forms a dominant motif in its retelling. That motif is persecution or, more fully construed, the faithfulness of the Saints despite persecution. One of the great turning points occurred in 1838. Let's take a look.

Even impartial historians would refer to the troubles between Mormons and their neighbors before 1838 as persecution of the Mormons. After that, however, "conflict" or even "mutual hostility" would be offered as more appropriate language, but not by devout Mormons, who tell the version of the story that promotes their faith.

Here's what happened. The Saints had moved, fleeing persecution, from Independence, Missouri, to Far West, Missouri, where they formed their own settlement. On July 4, 1838, LDS leader Sidney Rigdon made a rather inflammatory sermon, referred to as an "Extermination Oration," in which, based on prophetic assurances that God would give them this land, he threatened a war to exterminate any Missourians who would "disturb" the Mormons. Mormons actually attacked and plundered some non-Mormon settlements in the area about three months later. The governor, Lilburn Boggs, reciprocated Rigdon's speech, saying the Mormons had "made war" and "must be treated as enemies"; he issued an "extermination order."

The situation climaxed on October 30 in a terrible incident known as the Haun's Mill Massacre. At this Mormon site about fifteen miles from Far West, two hundred Missouri militiamen swooped in with guns blazing as women and children fled screaming into the woods and men and boys sought refuge in the blacksmith's shop. The shop became a death trap in which seventeen were killed and fifteen more were badly wounded; all were stripped of their valuable possessions. The mourning women and children dumped the bodies of their men into a nearby well as a makeshift grave. The very next day, three thousand Missouri militiamen surrounded the eight hundred Mormons at Far West and forced them to surrender and leave the state immediately.

Not surprisingly, this tragic incident and many other similar ones left a tremendously profound feeling of "We are a persecuted people" in the bones of Latter-day Saints. That feeling is still there, showing up in extreme sensitivity to attack in any form. Conversations that include any element of questioning by a non-Mormon, disparaging remarks, jokes that slight them—almost always these will be perceived as a form of attack on them for their faith, as just one more persecution, whether intended or not. That's why what I often thought was a mere discussion, my Mormon friends perceived as a "Bible bash."

3. The Death of Joseph Smith (1844)

The Saints fled to Nauvoo, Illinois, a swampy site on the Mississippi, where they made a settlement through hard work, dedication, and industry, which the neighbors admired. But the admiration stopped when news emerged about the four-thousand-man Nauvoo Legion, an army Joseph Smith had mustered that was nearly half the size of the standing army of the United States, and about Smith and a few other Mormon leaders having begun the practice of polygamy. In June of 1844, a Nauvoo paper published a story on the suddenly unsecret practice of polygamy. Smith had the press destroyed by the Legion, then fled from justice until he and his brother Hyrum and two others were arrested and jailed in Carthage, Illinois. On June 27, the Illinois militia sent to "protect" these prisoners actually stormed the jail instead! Joseph fired into the mob before jumping out of a second-floor window into a hail of bullets that killed him.

He was and is today considered a martyr by the Mormon people. This of course not only heroized him but also exacerbated the feeling of persecution at the core of Mormon cultural identity. And the death of the Mormons' "founding prophet" fueled their resolve and faithfulness to the cause as nothing else could have. Indeed, Mormon historian Will Bagley uses an astounding comparison in speaking of the imprint left in Mormon consciousness by this event:

> Joseph Smith's murder in the Carthage Jail in June, 1844, is the defining moment in Mormonism. In Mormon belief and society, the martyrdom of Joseph Smith is as important as the crucifixion, in terms of its meaning and power to people. The Mormon enemies believed that if they chopped off the head, the body would die. But in fact, by murdering Joseph Smith, the Mormons' enemies ensured that they would have a powerful and enduring religious tradition.[2]

4. The Trek West (ca. 1847)

Brigham Young, who inherited the prophethood after Smith, earned from historians the title of "the great American colonizer." At only forty-three years of age, under threats of impending arrest by Illinois authorities in January 1846, this great visionary and tireless leader began in February of that year to lead the Mormons on a massive migration westward. To build the new "Zion," they would have to leave the territorial United States, he determined. So on July 24, 1847, he and his party arrived in the Great Basin, where he declared in words that would become famous, "This is the place." Nearly one hundred thousand of the faithful followed him. They founded Salt Lake City and more than a hundred other towns in the next ten years, expanding north and south in an endeavor to establish their own country, a theocratic kingdom of Latter-day Saints! It was called the State of Deseret and ranged from parts of today's Idaho all the way south to San Bernardino.

This migration has left its imprint on Mormon culture today as an enormously celebrated symbol. In Utah, July 24 is more roundly celebrated than July 4! The locals seem to view themselves historically as Mormons first, Americans second. This is because, as historian Will Bagley puts it, "The Mormon migration to the West in 1847 becomes as powerful a story for the Mormon people as the Exodus is for the Jews."[3]

5. Polygamy and Its "Abolition" (1890)

The distinctive marriage practice of polygamy became the most obvious symbol setting Mormons apart from "Gentiles" (as non-Mormons were called by Mormons). It also caused tremendous tensions between the growing Mormon theocracy and the U.S. government, especially at the end of the Mexican-American War (1848) when Utah and its surrounding territory became a U.S. acquisition.

In short, though Brigham Young was appointed governor, he was not trusted by federal representatives, and due to the practice of polygamy (now a "divine precept," according to Prophet Young), Utah was denied statehood when it applied in 1862. In addition to suspicion and national ridicule for the practice, the Mormons suffered legal harassment, political and economic pressure, and even military siege, which brought tremendous humiliation to them. Harsh laws were passed that declared the practice a felony, LDS leaders were imprisoned, and Mormon Church property was seized. Impassioned speeches were made in Congress denouncing slavery and polygamy as "the twin relics of barbarism." Finally in 1890, LDS President and Prophet Woodruff declared for the "temporal salvation" of the Church a manifesto that abolished polygamy as an official practice.

Only about 10 percent of Mormon males were polygamous, but all suffered from the fallout due to this practice. To this day, jokes and quips abound about polygamy as a distinctive of Mormons. It is a shameful, embarrassing ghost from the past for many LDS people who wish it had never happened.

6. Statehood (1896)

Finally, six years after the manifesto, Utah became the forty-fifth state in the Union. There was great celebration over the event, to the point that a huge American flag was draped on the wall of the brand-new Salt Lake City Temple.

The significance of this is the complete change of Mormon culture and community from being intentionally isolated—an "us versus them" posture—to being the quintessential American ethnic group!

7. The Open Priesthood (1978)

From very early pronouncements and revelations, the LDS Church declared African-Americans ineligible to hold the priesthood. Again, this posture brought great ridicule and unfavorable regard, especially from the African-American community in the United States after the civil rights movement of the 1960s. Moreover, the last half of the twentieth century would mark the latinization of the LDS Church, yet very few Latinos were priests. So many new members were being added in Mexico, Central America, and South America that in the late 1980s the day came when its Hispanic members outnumbered its North American members!

It's easy to see, therefore, why the biggest and most transformative hingepoint of the twentieth century for the LDS Church was the revelation of 1978, reportedly received by President and Prophet Spencer W. Kimball, declaring the priesthood open to qualified male Mormons of *all* races.

Critical outsiders (and some liberal Mormons), of course, saw the "prophecy" coming at an opportunistic moment in history when political expediency demanded it; the same criticism was leveled at the manifesto ending church-sanctioned polygamy. But in the interests of understanding Mormon culture, we should realize the consensus among faithful Mormons is to perceive this as one more evidence that "the heavens are open," so God can reveal needed, up-to-date things to his people through his prophets. This revelation about non-Anglos and the priesthood became a stunning reversal that greatly helped modernize and rehumanize the public image of the LDS Church.

Conclusions: Mormon Culture on the Wing

As we actually find it "in flight" today, what trajectories do we see in Mormon culture as a result of these historical roots? When we meet and develop friendships with LDS people, how will these trajectories show up?

As a first trajectory, we'll notice a decisive, ingrained *prophetic certainty*. This is due to the founding story of Joseph Smith's First Vision, which inaugurated "the latter days," as well as ongoing, hingepoint revelation stories, especially the manifesto on polygamy and the statement on males of all races being accepted into the priesthood. Our LDS friends will typically have a very basic and unassailable trust in exclusive LDS claims to divinely authored modern revelation: because the prophets have divine authority, it's wrong to question them. This certainty trumps and defuses any argument that LDS prophets and their revelations contradict each other or the Bible. There will be a certainty about the heavens being "open" and God speaking to humans today, but *only* through the LDS Church—the only "restored" and "true" church of Jesus Christ in these "latter days"—and its prophets. Furthermore, Smith's vision shows that the LDS Church has "more truth" than merely Bible-based churches, so at the risk of some condescension, our Mormon friends will usually feel they have the same truth as traditional Christians but much more of it—for example, the "new truth" (again, from the First Vision) showing Heavenly Father is really an exalted man limited to a human body.

The second trajectory is a *persecution complex*. As noted, the Mormons' identity as a "persecuted people" from early on in their history is very deeply felt. Its imprint leaves Mormons today thin-skinned, hypersensitive, and virtually expecting to be attacked. And let's be plain: the major body of attackers then and now has been perceived as Protestant Americans. So as we saw, we may typically expect a defensiveness that quickly throws walls up at even the slightest critical questioning of any aspect of their religion and culture. One classic manifestation of this complex is the insulated, fixed Mormon aversion to any form of what gets labeled "anti-Mormon literature"—books and pamphlets critical of their history or teachings or personal-journey stories of people who leave the LDS Church. Do any of this, or any joking or ridiculing, as you relate to a believing Mormon, and you can plan to lose an audience for the gospel right then and there. It will be seen as "one more attack."

Third and last is a trajectory we might call the *exodus community*. Mormons' heroic perseverance despite hardships as they fled conflict and made the trek west both isolated them and melded them into a very strong community. Still today, Mormons are known for their great community cooperation and help-one-another ethic.

Attached to these roots and wings (history and trajectory) we find, as in any culture, a set of beliefs. We'll look at those next.

For Discussion and More

1. Tell about the history and tradition of your "people." Maybe you could write down a sketch of your family's "roots" or those of your ethnic group and explain it. For example, if your forebears were Dutch or Sudanese or Vietnamese immigrants, or maybe Tories in the American Revolution, recount the story and how this might have impacted you.

2. Perhaps you also could add the faith dimension and tell the spiritually significant version of your "people's" story. If they became traditional Christians, for example, two or three generations before you, tell how this happened and how it affects your testimony. See if you can share this, when appropriate, with a Mormon friend.

3. How might we sympathetically identify with "a persecuted people"? In what ways does the history of the Israelites in Egypt or under the Roman oppressors at the time of Jesus give us a way of talking with LDS people about how God feels our sufferings and loves to set us free?

4. Tease out some implications of Will Bagley's claim about the killing of Joseph Smith being "the defining moment in Mormonism" and "as important as the crucifixion, in terms of its meaning and power to people." How do traditional Christian martyr stories speak powerfully to us? How does this relate to the crucifixion of Christ?

5. What strategies might you devise to go beyond the "prophetic certainty" roadblock? Are there ways of conversing and dialoguing that can help LDS people appreciate the authority of the Bible, especially the authority of Jesus as "the Word made Flesh"?
6. What books or other materials (e.g., films and DVDs) might you consider giving to believing Mormons? What resources would you *not* consider giving to them?

4

Mormon Theology 101

The Template of Official Beliefs

Somewhere near the center of any culture we find a belief structure, the culture's agreed-on assertions about what is true concerning God, ourselves, and the world around us. In a highly religious culture like Mormonism, the structure looks like a set of religious doctrines. We'll examine this cultural piece here.

Are You Singing My Song?

As we begin, let me use a metaphor. If stating the doctrinal beliefs of the culture is like singing its theme song, Mormons can sound very much like they "sing the same song" as traditional Christians. Do they?

Well, there's a component we experience in the LDS "composition" that most certainly *is* the same. It's a bit like an experience I had in a remarkably "rainbow" (racially, sexually, economically diverse) San Francisco church very unlike my own. They sang "Amazing Grace" with the same old familiar tune I've known from childhood, so my sentimentality was quickly on board—but they made a small change in the lyrics by replacing "saved a wretch like me" with "saved *someone* like me." When I sang it, something seemed out of sync. Yes, it was the same song, but *no, it wasn't!* Therapeutically pleasing it might have been, but it was a cop-out! It no longer said the same thing converted slave trader John Newton meant to say when he wrote it and also to have us saying when we sing it.

Perhaps this experience furnishes us with a parallel to the experience of hearing and understanding standard Mormon doctrine. When LDS friends "sing" words like "The Lord Jesus Christ is my Savior" or "We must repent and have faith in the Lord Jesus," it sounds like they are singing the same song we are—until we listen more closely and find there are some changes that effectively make it a different song (at least in standard, official Mormonism).

One change occurs in word sameness with meaning differences, as in terms like *Heavenly Father, faith, repentance, gospel, salvation,* and *Lord Jesus Christ.* These words, held in common between traditional Christians and LDS people, are assigned different meanings by the two different groups. So, for example, in traditional Christian (or orthodox) belief, *Heavenly Father* refers to the invisible Creator and Sustainer of all he made, a Spirit everywhere present at once, all-knowing and all-powerful and in these ways utterly unlike what humans can ever be. In official Mormon belief, *Heavenly Father* has referred to a humanoid being limited to a physical body like ours but with exalted powers. (Note, however, this view of a physical, limited, humanoid "Father" is not highlighted in LDS literature today—often not even mentioned—although it was historically standard teaching until as late as 1992. Some official teaching is under revision or suppression. Appendix 2 gives some interesting documentation of such doctrinal changes.)

Another change in the "song" occurs with simple word difference—words used by Mormons that are unique to Mormon doctrine. For example, they use the terms *endowment*, *baptism for the dead*, *spirit prison*, and *Telestial Kingdom*, none of which typically occurs in traditional Christian pulpits or Sunday school classes. (If you're curious, check the glossary at the back of the book.)

A third change in the "song" occurs due to rhetoric (word sameness, *rhetorical* difference)—how the words are used to move us, and specifically how they are used by Mormons in ways that differ from how traditional Christians use them. This is not exactly the same as a difference in dictionary definition. A classic example is the use of a Book of Mormon text called "the promise of Moroni," which states in its most important part, "Ask God . . . if these things are not true . . . he will manifest the truth of it unto you, by the power of the Holy Ghost" (Moroni 10:3–5). The prospective convert is told by a Mormon missionary or friend simply to read the Book of Mormon and do what the words say, asking with a sincere heart, and God will answer. But the rhetoric, when decoded, is saying more than the mere words—three things more: (1) if the Book of Mormon is true, it automatically means Joseph Smith was a true prophet of God and the LDS Church is "the one true church"; (2) the way God tells you it is true is by a feeling you get called a "burning in the bosom," which is taken to come from the Holy Ghost; and (3) if you are sincere, God always and only answers in the affirmative—the corollary being that if you did not get a "yes" answer, you were insincere.

Such are the challenges we face in understanding how words get used to express Mormon theology. But the words are just the small bits, like individual pieces of a thousand-piece jigsaw puzzle. They need a context—a big picture, a worldview—in which to be made intelligible. So this chapter, while too brief a space to spell out the full A-to-Z of Mormon theology, is intended to introduce you to the big picture, the forest view, the fully assembled jigsaw puzzle. That big picture is known as the concept of Eternal Progression.

Notice how in this chapter I'm using terms like *standard* and *official* to characterize the Mormon doctrines we're studying. These teachings have been adhered to for most of the history of the Mormon Church, and on the church-sanctioned, official level, they still are. Incidentally but importantly, you should know my source: this material on Mormon doctrine comes from the official, currently used LDS Church teaching text entitled *Gospel Principles* (*GP*). You may order the book or find a link to the material on the website of Salt Lake Theological Seminary (www.slts.edu).

How God Became God: The Plan

The short version of this overarching doctrinal framework, the Plan of Eternal Progression (also called the Plan of Salvation), is classically summarized in a famous couplet by the fifth prophet of the LDS Church, Lorenzo Snow: "As man is, God once was; as God is, man may become." In very simple terms, this is saying the person Mormons call Heavenly Father was once a human just like us and simply worked his way up! That's how he became a god. (The Holy Ghost and the Son are also understood to be divine.) Furthermore, the couplet teaches that every human being can do the same thing *if* we do the *right* thing—that is, if we are obedient to "the gospel" of Mormonism with our lives. That's why Mormons understand humans to be what they call "gods in embryo"—the very stuff of godhood, with the innate ability to transform ourselves. But the progression of each of us occurs in three very distinct phases of existence, as follows.

1. *Premortal Existence* (also simply called "Preexistence"). This phase is known as the First Estate. Mor-

mons are taught to believe human life starts before our physical conception on earth. In heaven, our previous home, we were the literal offspring of a physical mother and father who are gods; we were born there, due to their sexual union, as spirit children. We were given talents and also had to make choices, mainly to obey the laws of the universe (just like Heavenly Father did and must keep doing), in order to "become perfected" and thus reach our potential. The heavenly parents want us to reach our potential and become gods because they want to share their joy with us.

If we are now on earth, we chose well. Becoming perfected entails the need to leave heaven's home for a while, be clothed with a body and live obediently on earth, then return with a resurrected body to continue our progress in heavenly life.

But there was a fly in the ointment: our weakness on earth would cause us to sin. Heavenly Father knew this and took action. In a "Grand Council" he declared his plan to us, according to which we would be tested on earth but would also need a Savior, which he would provide. He then called for someone he could send as the Savior and got responses from potential candidates. Jesus, also called Jehovah, was one, and his brother Satan, also called Lucifer, was the other. Each offered his salvation plan: Jesus offered to give his life for humans who could then choose salvation and progress, while Satan offered to *force* all humans to be saved. Heavenly Father accepted Jesus for the mission, at which point Satan led a rebellion, and a war in heaven ensued. Rebellious spirits were cast out with Satan and became demons to tempt us on earth; valiant spirits (we who chose well by aligning ourselves with Jesus) would progress through earthly life.

2. *Mortal Existence.* In this, the Second Estate, we enter earth through human parents chosen for us. Since this is a time of testing as to whether we will live obediently by faith and prove worthy, our memory of our preexistent life

in heaven by necessity is erased, or "veiled" from us. Here
we must, to use the popular Mormon slogan, "choose the
right" to continue our progression.

What exactly must we choose to "choose the right"? We
must follow a threefold path including not only the basics
of the gospel but also the "laws and ordinances of the
gospel." First the basics (called "first principles") must be
embraced, which are faith in Jesus Christ and repentance.
Second, there are rituals, which are called ordinances;
they include baptism (by LDS priests only), the laying on
of hands to receive the Holy Ghost (again, by LDS priests
only), receiving temple endowments, and temple marriage
(or "sealing"). Third, a host of laws, or commandments,
must be obeyed, which include among many others such
items as loving and worshipping God, living the law of
chastity, loving our neighbor, paying tithes and offerings,
being honest in all our dealings, obeying the Word of Wisdom (no coffee, tea, alcohol, or tobacco), and hearing and
following the inspired words of God's prophets.

One more crucial piece in this threefold path of choosing to live right is the concept of "worthiness"—and more
precisely, "temple worthiness"—which gets embodied in
the practice of "worthiness interviews." For LDS people
the notion of worthiness is very practical, measurable, and
attainable—not just a vaguely defined term of spirituality.
Starting from the goal and working backward, it looks like
this: to attain the Celestial Kingdom and godhood in the
next Estate (the afterlife), one must do temple works; to
do temple works, one must be "temple worthy," signified
by getting a ticket to enter the temple, called a "temple
recommend" (literally a small, official card); to get a recommend, one must pass a "worthiness interview" held
usually by one's bishop (the leader—like a pastor—of a
local "ward" or congregation); to pass a worthiness interview, one must *live* worthy and be able to substantiate it,
according to seven specific criteria. Some of the criteria
are, for example, being current on your tithe, keeping the

Word of Wisdom, being morally clean (law of chastity), and sustaining (voting to approve) the Church's authorities. Note in passing something very important here: there is no shortcut to, or getting around the necessity of, temple works in order to further your progression and attain godhood—even if some of them are done "by proxy" on your behalf by someone else!

3. *Post-mortal Existence.* Called the Third Estate, post-mortal existence presents to us the possibility of going to one of three "kingdoms of glory." After death, we enter an intermediate state as spirits—either "paradise," which holds the righteous, or "spirit prison" (also called "hell"), which holds the unrighteous who now have a second chance to choose Mormonism. Eventually all humans are resurrected, regaining their bodies, by the power of Christ's resurrection.

Then the Last Judgment is held, assigning each of us with our resurrected body to one of the three kingdoms, depending on our choices and worthiness record from earth life. The "Telestial Kingdom" (the lowest of the three) is prepared for non-LDS people, including even the wicked of the world; it is visited by angels and the Holy Spirit, but never Heavenly Father and the Son. The "Terrestrial Kingdom" (middle) is prepared for honorable non-LDS people, including converts from spirit prison; the Son of God visits here. The "Celestial Kingdom" (highest) is prepared for LDS people only and contains within it three levels. Only at the top level do Heavenly Father and the Son live, along with Mormons who were married in the temple, and only there can one finally move on to be exalted to godhood; those in the lower two levels serve those in the top level.

Let me insert here a big-picture statement about the "big picture" we've just looked at. Though this question is rather futile, some ask: where did all this get started? Or put another way, who's the original god who started this whole process? The answer I heard given by a very fine, very informed, and articulate instructor at an LDS Institute of Religion was as good as I've heard anywhere. He simply said, "It's an eternal round." That is, according to standard Mormonism, the process called Eternal Progression has no beginning and will have no end.

The above, in short, describes the Mormon Plan of Salvation, or Eternal Progression. It functions, as a friend and colleague of mine likes to say, like the string holding all the beads on a necklace together—all the individual beliefs make sense only when "strung together" with this overarching doctrine.

A Few Strategic Trees in the Forest

Having looked at the forest, let's now focus on a few of the trees or, better, forest glens where it may be worth our while to give special attention, special dwelling time. They deserve special attention because they are strategic focal points for our discussions with Mormon friends—"discussions" that begin with our listening attentively to them at these points and continue with our wise and gentle, biblically informed responses. I see four of these strategic areas of doctrine that not only are helpful for our understanding of the Mormon "song" but also may be used as a kind of template for LDS people who are at the stage of wanting to discuss doctrinal issues. These are not in any order of importance, just key issues.

One issue is, *what kind of god is God?* It makes an enormous difference whether we are dealing with a god who is not essentially different from us (made of the same "stuff") and must obey the same cosmic laws as we to progress, or with a God who differs radically from us and contains qualities of being and powers we can never share. The former describes the gods of official Mormon doctrine (Heavenly Father, Jesus Christ, the Holy Ghost, and innumerable others): limited beings subject to other forces and laws, who worked their way up to godhood as entities who (in my take on this) remain part of a larger cosmic "machine" or "eternal round" to which they are subject. The latter begins to describe the biblical notion of God: the Creator of all; subject to nothing and no one outside himself; omnipotent, omniscient, and omnipresent (not limited to a body); and yet personal and "closer than a brother" to each one of us. (Consider texts like Genesis 1; Isaiah 44; and Acts 17.) This distinction makes a difference because the first kind of being may rightly evoke admiration and emulation while the second kind rightly evokes contrite-hearted worship and obedience from an unmitigated creature (and a fallen, needy one at that).

A simple anecdote may help here. It comes from a friend who was formerly a Mormon. On his mission in England, he came to a door where a charming lady answered. After he and his mission partner offered greetings and introductions, they did the usual prescribed inquiry regarding the woman's acquaintance, if any, with the LDS Church. Then she asked about God's relationship to the "laws and ordinances" of which they spoke. My friend answered with the stock LDS view, telling her God is subject to the same laws of the universe as we and had to follow them to be exalted to godhood. With complete innocence, grace, and utter noncombativeness, she stated in her lovely Queen's English, "Oh, that's strange—I would rather have thought God *made* the laws." The two politely dismissed themselves shortly after that comment and moved on in their contact work. My friend, however, reports this as his first major disturbance about Mormon theology, since he could not truly find himself at peace about a kind of god who is not superior to the laws of the universe. Though his disturbance went undetected by others at the time, he had just moved a major first step in the journey leading him eventually into traditional Christianity.

Sometimes I have used a similar suggestion in conversing with Mormon friends. I first describe, as best I understand it, the LDS Heavenly Father's position as one god among many in the Eternal Progression "round" or cosmic machine. I then pause to ask if they think I've accurately described official LDS teaching on this, to which they've always responded in the affirmative. Then I offer for the sake of discussion to grant the Eternal Progression plan as valid and ask them to imagine something, or rather, Some*one*: what if there were another Being *outside and above* the whole "round" who made it all and made the laws by which it operates—you know, a kind of *"God* god"? Usually I'll see them caught a bit short, pause, or get big eyes and say, "That would be a very different, much bigger kind of God." I will then simply ask them to consider the God of the Bible as Someone roughly like that, at least for a beginning image.

A second issue is, *what kind of Jesus is Jesus?* Here we will want to discuss just what we can know about Jesus from the story of his life. If we simply assume the playing field is our common commitment to the New Testament Gospels as our source, it's a pretty even playing field. We'll want to focus on just who he is and what he came to do. Is he another limited god, or God the Son who is yet as fully human as any one of us except for being even more human due to his sinlessness (for sin diminishes our humanity)? Did he come to pay for our salvation in full—the meaning of his words "It is finished"—or only in part?

A third issue is, *what really is grace all about?* I think here it is helpful not just to define the term and put it in the context of salvation but also to talk about how we experience God's grace. Classic definitions can be good, like "unmerited favor" or "the unconditional, undeserved, and unexpected gift of God's mercy and love." Mormons are taught that grace is conditional; it is God's empowerment "after all we can do," a Book of Mormon text says (more on this later). Verses like Ephesians 2:8–10 are good to quote. But images and experiences of grace that make it palpable are the most powerful ways to talk about it with Mormon friends.

One great source to use is the parables of Jesus and stories of encounters he had with others where grace was given them. I love to retell the very short story about the Pharisee and the tax collector going to the temple to pray, painting the character sketches of each one and noticing their actions carefully: how stunning that the one who was bankrupt of spirit and brokenhearted so that he called out for mercy was justified! Here it's important to stress the picture of us in our sin as one of abject, helpless poverty or destitution of spirit—not just a person going from good to better. Or how about the "sinful" woman who crashes the dinner party at Simon the Pharisee's house where Jesus is the honored guest (although Simon has refused to treat him with common, hospitable graces)—and she goes home with her sins forgiven!

Finally, a fourth issue is, *what kind of revelation from God is authoritative?* Another spin on this is simply the old question, "Can we trust the Bible?" LDS people use the Bible, and yet official Mormon teaching puts its authority under suspicion by claiming it has been corrupted through translation error. The "uncorrupted" authority sources they are taught to trust above the Bible are the three standard works of LDS scripture (the Book of Mormon, Doctrine and Covenants, and Pearl of Great Price) and also the living prophet who heads the LDS Church.

In very rare circumstances, it may help to discuss reasons traditional Christians find the Bible trustworthy—excellent ancient manuscripts, study of what the text clearly says in its original languages (thus getting "behind" translation problems), God's intent to speak clearly to us and not "stutter," universal agreement among traditional Christians about what the core of the Bible teaches, and so on. Those rare circumstances include formal scholarly discussion or presentations or the case of someone with a genuine attitude of inquiry who takes the initiative to ask us questions about this issue. Generally these circumstances do not apply, however, in which case my normal practice is just to use the Bible as common ground and assume its authority. Most LDS people have a residual reverence for the Bible's authority or at least a high respect for it that functions in much the same way. Regardless of this, God uses his Word as he promised whenever it is proclaimed, so we cannot lose when we quote it and ground our statements with it.

Conclusions

As we bring this chapter to an end and anticipate the next, we need to consider the role of theological understanding in relating to our Mormon friends. Usually theology is not a good starting point; the exception is when our LDS friend or acquaintance takes the initiative to ask us to "go there." Normally, a study of their doctrine and ours has value in helping us listen and be attuned to the shape and tones and textures of the "song" they've been taught to sing, so we can better and more truly speak the biblical gospel into their world of understanding. But that world is not one-dimensional and monolithic. As we now turn to explore further how to make our theological understanding fruitful and practical, we'll see we need to come to terms with, among other things, the great diversity of the Mormon social and cultural world.

For Discussion and More

1. Think carefully about the role of theological understanding in the overall process of relating to the LDS people in your life. Discuss or reflect on both the advantages and disadvantages of this kind of knowledge in various circumstances. Whether it's the knowledge of orthodox Christian theology or of LDS theology, how can it be used to "build up" rather than to "puff up"?

2. Try an exercise in identifying the core message of both belief systems. First, state in one sentence the gospel according to traditional Christian teaching. Then, state in one sentence the gospel according to Mormon teaching.

3. Interview three or more LDS people, asking them to state "the gospel" in their own words, and second, to state what new beliefs you would have to adopt (if any) to join the LDS Church. If you are in a study group, share the answers you got, and synthesize them into some conclusions about what you've learned.

4. God, Jesus, grace, the Bible—on these four topics, how does Mormon doctrine differ from traditional Christian doctrine? Are there similarities between the two? Notice carefully how terms are used and words defined in each belief system.

5. Discuss what Scripture texts you find most helpful in understanding biblical teaching and explaining it to LDS friends.

5

101 Laboratory

The So-Whats of Discussing Theology with Mormons

If we know basic Mormon doctrine cold and, I hope, know biblical doctrine even better, well, so what? What does this buy us? What good will it do for our witness to Mormons? I raise such issues especially in light of these statements from Paul's famous love poem recorded in 1 Corinthians 13: "If I speak God's Word with power, revealing all his mysteries and making everything plain as day . . . but I don't love, I'm nothing. . . . Love . . . takes pleasure in the flowering of truth" (vv. 2, 4–5 Message).

Making Theology Count

Understanding LDS doctrine is one thing; dialoguing about doctrine with actual LDS people is another. Perhaps we know what we think and we know what they think; we may even know what we think about what they think, at least on some matters. But whatever the matters are, does it really *matter?* More precisely, we must ask ourselves, *"For what* does it matter, and *when* does it matter?"

Actually, rank-and-file Mormon people generally are unreflective about doctrinal or theological issues, just like the rank and file of many religious groups. Let's be honest: many traditional Christians are woefully unreflective too. This tendency may, in the case of Mormon people, be more extreme than in other cases because theologizing about faith is simply not an important value in their culture. Remember, they are heart people, not head people. Getting their doctrinal p's and q's correct takes a backseat to "getting a testimony" and "trusting the prophet." One can find exceptions to this in Mormon community, but very few. Predominantly, devotion gets valued and valorized far above scholarship, faith far above critical thinking. So when if at all does knowledgeable, clear, careful theological discussion with Mormon friends happen?

Don't get me wrong: the answer is not "never." But it's also not "always." The main point I'd like to hammer home in this chapter is that *we need to prayerfully seek and sensitively seize those doors of opportunity God grants us in which our theological knowledge truly counts.*

And what should it count *for?* Our objective is never just imparting knowledge about God (no matter how "correct") but helping people *know God.* We will want to harness our theological insights, then, to serve this objective, for in that way it becomes part of bringing the Bible's Good News to our LDS friends—not just giving them information on a picture postcard about the Artesian Well we've discovered but giving them the Water of Life! So, having the knowledge is not enough; articulating the knowledge well, even if we have "the tongues of men and of angels," is not enough; stellar comparisons of Mormon doctrine to biblical teachings, even if argued forcefully and with utmost clarity, is not enough. How we hold our theological knowledge and how we use it are the crucial concerns.

I recall a time when my wife and I, as newlyweds, lived in Denver. This was back when I was young and foolish and no small part of my modus operandi could be explained by my having just graduated from seminary. I could be justly accused of acting like I "had all the answers." A seminary classmate and I—in collusion with one another in this knowledge-mongering agenda—invited the Mormon missionaries over to my apartment. We got past the polite "Where are you from?" and "What's your family like?" talk and offered them hot chocolate that they gratefully accepted and quaffed—something we did well and I'd do again, by the way. And then we laid into them about their bad, unorthodox, heretical theology—God having a body of flesh and bones, the church going into total apostasy, Joseph Smith's claimed prophethood failing to pass the Bible's tests, blah, blah, blah. I'll never forget how calmly and unphasedly they responded by simply "bearing their testimony" about the LDS Church being the true Church and Joseph Smith being a true prophet *despite anything we said.* Nor will I ever forget my seminary friend's parting words as he shook hands with the missionaries: "Bye now. I hope to see you again. I'd like to see you in heaven—if you ever get your theology straightened out."

What we said that day may have been consummately knowledgeable, clear, and biblically truthful, but today I'm convinced it was not *biblically faithful.* How we held and used our correct biblical theology (to whatever extent we had it right, which may itself be questionable) was not faithful to how the Bible itself exhorts us to hold and use such knowledge; as we "give an answer" to anyone asking the reason for our hope, we must do so "with gentleness and respect" (1 Peter 3:15). It seems we were knowledge rich and wisdom poor, and I gravely doubt we were "speaking the truth in love," as Ephesians 4:15 exhorts.

Besides, even if the missionaries did "get their theology straightened out," would they by virtue of attaining theological correctness qualify for heaven? No, no, a thousand times no! John Wesley was an Anglican minister with all his orthodox theology intact for years before his heart was "strangely warmed" and he knew he was "born again." As he so compellingly learned, theology doesn't save—*God* saves (1 Peter 1:3–5)! And on our end of the process, what God calls for in us is not primarily, fundamentally, or crucially *doctrinal* knowledge but *personal* knowledge, not *theological truth* but *personal trust*. This personal act of trust, or faith, turns out to be more a heart matter than a head matter, even though a certain core of doctrinal truth about the biblical gospel is an important component of the decision (Jesus, God's Son, died in our place and rose again for us sinners, and this grace-gift alone can save us [Rom. 5:6–11; Eph. 2:8–10]). Doctrinal knowledge may be more crucial to our *understanding* what happens when God saves us than to God saving us.

Crucial or not, then, when does discussing theology with LDS people really count in a way that helps them toward the kingdom of God, and what must we do to prepare ourselves for those times?

The Ins and Outs of Discussing Theology with Mormons

We deal with an internal issue and also an external issue as we discuss doctrine with Mormon people. The internal issue concerns the spirituality of knowledge, or how our knowledge relates to our spiritual health and growth. "Knowledge puffs up," warns the apostle, "but love builds up" (1 Cor. 8:1). We are exhorted to "grow in the grace and knowledge of our Lord and Savior Jesus Christ" (2 Peter 3:18). Whether in practical or doctrinal matters, it seems knowledge in the New Testament view never stands alone, is never valued merely for its own sake. Rather we must hold it in the context of deeper marks of character—love and grace being noted above—and only use it in keeping with that character.

Among other things, our growth in godly (or Christlike) character means knowledge becomes the handmaiden of our love for people. Knowledge that "bears the beams of love" to people can be truly redemptive. God forbid our knowledge becomes a puffy display of our wit and expertise to our Mormon friends, instead of a means by which we genuinely love them and minister God's grace to them so they can find and know the God of the Bible! The internal issue, then, concerns how we hold the knowledge we have, and this, our spirituality of knowledge, will become the greatest determinant of how we use it in relationships with others. If we hold it *masterfully*, like a debater all studied up to win the argument, well, we may indeed win the argument, but that's all. Forget about winning the person to Christ. If we hold it *patronizingly*, like a grade-school grammar teacher drilling people we regard as ignorant until they "get it right," we'll probably just foster irritation, resentment, and even anger in our listeners. If we hold it *ashamedly*, though, as timid people who fear offending our Mormon friends by telling the truth of the Bible (especially when we know it might differ from their beliefs), we will be inauthentic to ourselves and unfaithful to our Lord, as well as unhelpful to any who really do need some divine light in their darkness. If, on the other hand, we hold our theological knowledge (the "divine light" we've been given so far) *humbly, gently, respectfully, lovingly,* and *graciously,* as the Scriptures mentioned before tell us to do, we'll embody a measure of spiritual growth in Christlikeness and no doubt find ourselves using that knowledge redemptively! In short, our internal spirituality will shape the external outworking of how we relate to the Mormon people God puts in our lives.

Externally, we deal with precisely this matter of when and how to wisely use our knowledge of doctrine, both biblical and Mormon, in relationship with our Mormon friends. As a general rule, to echo my main drumbeat in this chapter, *we discuss theology with Mormons, humbly*

and graciously, when God opens the door for it. I'm saying
the *when* becomes a matter of providential timing and the
how becomes a matter of serving in love with the gentle,
respectful, but clear expression of our knowledge.

To put it in a kind of cautionary frame, let's not run
ahead of God's opportune moments as we relate to our
Mormon friends, and when those moments come, let's be
sure we use our doctrinal knowledge not to puff up but
to build up. We'll look at this more extensively later, but
in short, these moments occur, for example, when your
LDS friend initiates by asking a doctrinal question (e.g.,
"Do you believe in deathbed repentance?" or "Does your
church believe people are born with original sin?"), when
an event brings a theological issue to the surface and it's
clear your friend wants to talk about it (e.g., a movie or
the death of a loved one), or when Mormon missionaries
come to your door and in their program for discussion
raise doctrinal issues.

Let me make two more short observations about the
external side of doctrinal discussion with LDS people. For
one, we need to major in the majors; in other words, let's
avoid rabbit trails. Judi Abdulla, a former Mormon, says it
cogently. In our witness to Mormons, after the importance
of praying for them (since no argument ever makes people
enter God's kingdom) comes the importance of focusing on
the most essential things, and the most essential things are
not polygamy, *not* the Word of Wisdom, *not* even Joseph
Smith.

> The most essential things, the things that keep Mormons
> out of the kingdom of heaven, have to do with the nature
> of God: Who is he? And who is Jesus Christ? Is Jesus my
> spirit brother, or is he God in the flesh? And then, who are
> we that we need Jesus Christ? Are we gods in embryo, able
> somehow to attain godhood through our own efforts, or
> are we helpless sinners and enemies of God that he loved
> and for whom he gave himself?[1]

My second observation concerns individuality among Mormons, and my counsel is simple: don't stereotype. Don't assume you know what your LDS friends believe. Ask them! Mormon culture (and community), although it looks monolithic, is considerably diverse in lifestyle and in belief. Not every Mormon accepts everything in standard Mormonism. Some Mormons don't believe humans are cut out to become gods and goddesses. More common in my own experience are those Mormons who simply don't care about that doctrine even if it is official LDS teaching; they cavalierly relegate it to some fuzzy afterlife issue not worthy of their attention now, since all they really want to do is get through this life with some success, respect, godliness, and moral uprightness. Many like part of the theological package and not other parts, so they have a pick-and-choose, designer Mormonism. A friend of ours was for years a well-loved, respected teacher in the LDS release-time education program. He accepted assignments to teach the Bible and the Book of Mormon, but never the Doctrine and Covenants (a more distinctively unorthodox part of LDS scriptures) because he simply did not believe much of its teaching. Some Mormons don't care about doctrine, period! They're in the LDS Church because of its health practices (keeps the kids off drugs, for example), family attachments, or other reasons.

Please, let's confess the truth: we traditional Christians have our own problems with choosiness and selectivity, so we have no room to look down our noses at LDS folk. I recall when a young couple in our congregation left to join a church in the Reformed tradition because ours failed to be Calvinistic enough for them. Years later, another young man left us for a Pentecostal church because we don't advocate speaking in tongues as something desirable for all Christians. We have denominations that give us lots of options for consumeristic, cafeteria-style faith. Mormons have fewer options, so they make their peace and live strategically within the system or in rarer cases join (or form) a splinter group outside the LDS Church that follows some variant of Mormon teachings. Both traditions—biblical Christian and Mormon—have the problems diversity brings.

The bottom line is this: find out where your particular friends are in their awareness and attitude toward standard LDS teachings and biblical teachings, find out what really motivates them, and go from there. To whatever extent you discuss doctrine, *if* you discuss doctrine, make it count! Pray, open doors of opportunity, and act gently and wisely.

Missionaries at Your Door

Let's take a longer look at some of those doors of opportunity we might sensitively open, and let's start with that missionaries-at-the-door scenario. Most of us have been there, I'd bet: two clean-cut young men wearing ties, white shirts, and black badges appear when you answer the doorbell's summons. "Hi," they say, "we're missionaries from the Church of Jesus Christ of Latter-day Saints. We're in your neighborhood today talking with people about Jesus Christ. Would you have a few minutes?" Right here you face a critical juncture, a moment in which you can choose to connect or not to connect with two human beings God cares about. I'm hoping you'll look past the badges and the starchy uniform right into their eyes and connect; in fact, I hope you'll be the most hospitable place they hit all day, all week, or maybe even in their whole two years. I'm hoping you'll connect, not mostly to learn about the LDS Church, but to learn about *them*.

My own style is to invite them in and offer them refreshments they'll enjoy, like lemonade or hot chocolate (sorry, that Michelob's out of the question) and perhaps some cookies. Then I try as soon and as much as possible to put things on a personal footing, asking permission to know their first names as we get acquainted ("Elder Christiansen" is so cold and stiff, after all) and moving through the introductory personal information with real interest as we exchange backgrounds with one another. I try to show more interest than most people they'll meet, finding out about their families, hobbies, favorite movies or books, girlfriends, and so on. At this point I may even express admiration for their commitment to spend two years in this kind of disciplined activity when so many of their generation get into drugs and other nonconstructive living patterns.

Then I sit back and prepare to listen to their prepared presentation—and listen with respect, for this is part of loving them. At this point, theological, doctrinal issues will arise from them, although the issues will be dressed in sales-presentation language. First I want to actively listen, showing genuine interest and asking questions to clarify and see how much their teachings connect with them as persons, doing my level best to avoid an attacking tone. I might ask such questions as, "Are the LDS prophets believed to be just like the Old Testament ones? How often do they give prophecies?" "Tell me, Hyrum, do you find it hard or easy to keep all the commandments of Jesus? Do you ever feel like you're not making it?" Then I like to simply respond with calmness and clarity, and without any defensiveness, when they ask their scripted questions to draw me in. Sometimes I tell a story or ask a return question of them.

Responding to their doctrinal issues will drive you, as it has me, to your knees and to the Scriptures, which is really not a bad thing for us. Some of their typical items are these, quoted directly from *"Preach My Gospel,"* the LDS missionary guide currently in use:

God is our Heavenly Father. We are His children. He has a body of flesh and bone that is glorified and perfected.[2]

With the death of the Apostles, priesthood keys and the presiding priesthood authority were taken from the earth. . . .

This apostasy eventually led to the emergence of many churches.[3]

Christ promises to forgive our sins on the condition that we accept Him by exercising faith in Him, repenting, receiving baptism by immersion, and the laying on of hands for the gift of the Holy Ghost, and striving faithfully to keep His commandments to the end of our lives.[4]

Christ's Church is built on the foundation of apostles and prophets, who direct the Church by revelation. The Lord called Joseph Smith as the first prophet and head of this last dispensation. His successors who lead The Church of Jesus Christ of Latter-day Saints today are also prophets and apostles.[5]

A discussion with LDS missionaries may go for a while before they come to the end of their program for that session. There are five basic lessons in the series and additional ones they are counseled to use on an "as the Spirit leads" basis. Thus the twosome will hope to visit your home at least five times—if you're responsive and willing to continue. Be aware that their program goal is not to teach but to baptize; indeed, as early as the second discussion, they may bring up baptism and are instructed to get the "investigators" (that's you) to agree to a date to be baptized into the LDS Church!

Knowing this agenda may help us sense what's coming and also what coaching and pressures our two new friends are under, and I do hope and pray we seek to make them friends. But also, it's entirely appropriate and advisable for us to have an agenda of our own. We have some options and also some things to realize. We may sit through the lessons as structured; we may learn, respond biblically, and share our witness of saving faith in Christ along the way, though we'll need to be honest about not being a candidate for baptism. We may propose an alternative agenda or even a "half theirs, half ours" division of time, in which for our part we perhaps study together some passages of the Bible (like the first three chapters of the Gospel of John). We may go beyond the living-room relationship and invite them to dinner and perhaps some events at our church or in the community—a worship service, a drama, a Christian concert, a social, or the like.

We must realize, though, that these young men (or in a minority of cases, women) are under supervision and pressure to reach their objectives—mainly, to baptize people—so they may be called to quit meeting with us and move on if they sense we're not a "prospect." Sometimes just one "companion" of the two is directed to move on and will be replaced by someone else. Our commitment is simple: we meet with them all we can, love them all we can, respect them all we can, and express our relationship with Christ all we can, as long as God gives us an open door. A marvelous example of a successful long-term ministry like this is found in the case study of the Murphys in Appendix 3. While that door is open, we want to engage in doctrinal discussion only as far as it is helpful, usually as a response to what our LDS friends are claiming or asking. We always speak clearly and sensitively, never argue, in a way that can be used to let our Lord move them toward his kingdom.

"I'm Thinking of Becoming a Mormon"

If you hear words like these on the lips of a friend, co-worker, family member, or member of your church, be grateful she trusts you enough to talk with you about it. This comment may signal the door is still open to hear an alternative.

Of course you'll want to ask why she is thinking of making this move and find out the circumstances and persons influencing her. If, for example, the major reason she is considering the move is due to a romantic relationship with a Mormon person, she may be more locked in than she's letting on; and of course, the issue will probably not be dealt with by discussing the doctrines, since the real pull is more emotional than doctrinal. "Love is blind" in more ways than one.

But in many cases this kind of door offers a chance for fruitful study and discussion of the teachings of the LDS Church in light of the Bible. If your friend is willing to do this, help her take a good, serious look at the comparisons, and pray a lot for her and with her about discovering God's truth. Look at LDS sources, and clarify the core of the religion, articulated in the previous chapter of this book, as well as a few of the major issues. The core, remember, is the Eternal Progression doctrine in which LDS people are taught God was once a man and humans can progress to become gods. Other major issues might include, as also mentioned in the previous chapter, who God is, who Jesus Christ is, what it means to be human, and what grace really means for us in terms of salvation. Clarify the Bible's teachings, and pray for God's Spirit to use you.

"I'm Questioning My Mormon Beliefs"

Those stating this—Mormons who may be thinking about leaving the Mormon Church—are also trusting you a great deal, and you don't want to violate or diminish that trust. Gently find out what specific beliefs they are questioning, and go from there. Express how the Bible responds to the issues they talk about, and sympathize with them by recognizing how difficult a process this may be for them. Beyond that, my counsel is basically the same as pertains to those thinking of joining the LDS Church (as discussed earlier): look at the teachings in question in light of the Bible's teachings, and pray for God to reveal his truth. Also, invite these Mormon friends to a Bible-based church where they can hear good biblical teaching and preaching and experience the worship. A lifelong-LDS, thirtysomething woman who was inactive and questioning her beliefs visited our church several years ago at the invitation of my wife, Hazel, and myself. When I asked for her response to the service, she said something quite powerful: "Since I was a child, I've always had a certain image, sort of like a recurring dream, of what a community of people would be like if the Spirit of God was in them. What I experienced today was just like my dream image!"

"What Did You Think of What Happened at the ___?"

Many events can become open doors—and not only events held by traditional Christians but also ones produced by Mormons. Yes, invite your LDS friends to your church, to a special concert, to a film with Christian significance, to a social or campout or retreat with a parachurch group. Be resourceful! Then discuss with them what they saw and heard. But go as well to events on Mormon turf, your Mormon friends' comfort zone, and discuss with them what you observe. Go to an LDS promotional film or stage event, to a special seasonal concert at their ward, to a neighborhood party they host. Ask questions and learn. This too can become a real open door, because at times discussions of doctrine may rise to the surface, understanding can increase for everyone involved, and you can respectfully share your witness.

A few years ago, some dear LDS friends of ours invited us to tour the new Mormon temple in a neighboring town, Bountiful. Mormon temples are open to the public when first constructed or freshly renovated, and *only* then—a major public relations event. Tours through the building are conducted for a certain number of days before the temple is closed, consecrated, and then used only for secret ceremonies only worthy Mormons may attend. We joined our friends, another couple about our age, and went through the tour with them. Since then we've discussed lots of questions, given them a contemporary translation of the Bible (which the husband often carries to church), and discussed issues of doctrine with them many times. As I write, they've just enthusiastically accepted an invitation to go with us to hear Ravi Zacharias speak in the Salt Lake Tabernacle on "Jesus Christ as the Way, the Truth and the Life" (a historic occasion, since the last time a non-Mormon preacher spoke there was in 1899).

Four Door Closers

But not all ways of discussing doctrine are helpful to our witness. We traditional Christians make real mistakes (and close doors) sometimes. We ought to be aware of the following four mistakes.

The first I'll call *preachery*. This problem occurs when we view Mormons as two-dimensional information processors who simply need to have their bad information replaced by our good information. If we can just correct their doctrine, we reason, we've served our purpose and "ministered" to them. We figure their need is simply to get free of the in- culcated heresy and unorthodox theology of Mormonism by filling up their minds with the good, orthodox, biblical doctrine we're anxious to dump on them or proclaim at them. And indeed, you'll find that those given over to this approach typically have a modus operandi of dumping on and proclaiming at. Very little true dialogue takes place, even less listening, and marginal-to-zero friendship build- ing. We may be dumping, but they aren't loading, so the result is like water running off a duck's back.

A second door closer committed by traditional Chris- tians is what I'd call *taunting*. Really we're talking here about a more extreme, negative, in-your-face version of preachery. It occurs regularly in the leaflets and on the streets (and by the way, those leaflets often end up on the streets) of Salt Lake City. In the downtown plaza, loud-mouthed, denunciatory street preachers have been making the news as I write. They taunt, ridicule, and condemn the LDS Church and its doctrines, often at the top of their lungs. It makes headlines but not converts.

A third mistake is *dilettantism*. This refers to the enterprise of holding theological discussions ad infinitum to simply gain all manner of refined understanding of one another's beliefs. It may build some civility by respectful dialogue between Mormons and traditional Christians, which does have some real value, but it can also end up in a quagmire of polite intellectualizing that is more about salving curiosity than seeking truth. And nothing changes.

Let's call the fourth and last mistake *avoidance*. Sometimes out of fear, sometimes out of ignorance, private habits ("I never wear my religion on my sleeve"), "propriety," or other tendencies, we simply avoid the issue; in fact, we avoid every issue involving us in discussions of doctrine. We just never bring up matters of doctrine, and we don't respond when others bring them up. We steadfastly refuse to "go there." While this may be socially safe, it may also cause us to disobey God when he opens a door for us to "go there" and expects us to make this part of our witness.

A Living Example

A friend of mine named Marvin Anderson, who enjoys relationships with LDS people, has had many encounters with their missionaries. He told me about a question that comes up from time to time, namely, "Are Mormons Christians?" It's a current hot button between Mormons and traditional Christians.

Marv explained that when this question comes up, it's usually preceded by one of the missionaries talking about the refusal of many other kinds of Christians to accept Mormons as Christians. The missionary then asks him

point-blank, "Do *you* believe we're Christians?" Marv has
a wonderfully gentle but forthright way of deflecting the
force of this sensitive question by bringing up a doctrinal
point in response. His response goes to the core of the
issue, which is the theological belief concerning what a
Christian actually *is*, but Marv makes this response with
the shoe on the other foot—that is, from the LDS point
of view. In effect, he uses the rabbinic method of Jesus by
answering a question with a question.

First, Marv cites a basic biblical teaching and a teaching
about priesthood authority, one of the basic Mormon doctrines, by stating, "As I understand it, we both believe Paul
the apostle said in Romans 8:9 that if anyone does not have
the Spirit of Christ, he or she does not belong to Christ; in
other words, he or she is not a Christian. But the LDS doctrine about this [specifically, the LDS Articles of Faith—see
appendix 1 for the text of these] says the only way I can get
the Spirit of Christ (the Holy Ghost) into my life is to be
baptized and have 'the laying on of hands to receive the Holy
Ghost.' Both acts must be performed by a Mormon with
priesthood authority, or they don't have any divine power
and aren't valid. Do I understand that correctly?"

"Yes," the missionary will say (because Marv has obviously done his homework).

Then Marv will raise his rabbinic question: "Then it
would seem to me, my friends, that if you believe the LDS
Church's doctrine on this, you'd have to believe *I* am not
a Christian, since I've never had that done to me. Is that
your belief?"

Of course this approach turns the tables and may leave
our Mormon friends on the hot seat, but that's not where
we want them left. Nor does Marv. Rather, we want our
friends to become prepared, open, and a bit curious about
the main issue we'll want to talk about next. We may then
suggest, "Why don't we look together at some more of the
statements of Jesus and the apostles about what a Christian is and how one becomes a Christian?"

This kind of engaging and informed witness, driven by love, will leave an indelible, divine mark in the souls of LDS family and friends, again because we will have been faithful, effective, and sensitive in how we discuss doctrine in the context of building a relationship. As we now turn to see, some of these family members and friends will come to Christ and move beyond Mormonism.

For Discussion and More

1. The Scripture text quoted at the head of this chapter says, "Love . . . takes pleasure in the flowering of truth." How do you think we can develop a pleasurable, non-contentious way of exploring truth with our Mormon friends—a way that embodies and exudes love? Have you learned from models who do this well?
2. The seduction of discussing theology often is the gaining of mastery through knowledge: it's heady stuff to know lots of doctrine—both theirs and ours—and have the expertise to "set people straight." Just so, warns Scripture, "Knowledge puffs up." How shall we build a spirituality of knowledge that can resist this seduction and tell the truth of good doctrine, even correcting bad doctrine (yes, theirs *and* ours), in a way that "builds up" because it truly serves our love and God's love for all of us?
3. Invite some LDS missionaries over to your house. Use any local Church of Jesus Christ of Latter-day Saints listing in the yellow pages to request them. Tell them you wish to get to know them and learn about their church through their lessons and also wish to explore matters of faith from the Bible if they'd be willing. See where it leads. Pray for and look for that "open door."
4. What kinds of events might you see as good avenues for building a relationship with Mormons and open-

ing up possibilities for dealing with spiritual and theological issues? Brainstorm, then perhaps pick one or two and actually try it out with a Mormon friend or friends.

5. In your own experience, have you seen some of the mistakes that become door closers operating among traditional Christians? Are there other mistakes you could name? What steps can we take to replace them with more positive approaches?

6

Mormons in Transition

The Travels and Travails

Some Latter-day Saints—even lifelong members—have a change of heart and mind, leading them to journey out of Mormonism. The change may result from any of several different causes. No single cause, as we'll see, fits everyone. Some have a deeply emotional epiphany, some a crisis of ethics, some a quiet desperation over failure to live up to the LDS Church's standards, some a deliberate and reasoned reevaluation of the Church's teachings or history or practices. Whatever the cause or causes, these people feel the Mormon Church did not provide what they need.

Some of these former Mormons move into traditional Christianity, its faith and its variegated community, and that's what we're interested in for this chapter. Often those who make this kind of transition face some travails, some hardships, some painful adjustments due not only to leaving the LDS Church and its culture but also to entering traditional Christian circles. They may take the journey of leaving their church, but they do not take it lightly.

Breakin' Up Is Hard to Do

What makes this transition so hard? Maybe it's a bit like breaking up with your girlfriend or boyfriend when you're in high school, but on a much deeper level and with more serious ramifications. After all, in this case your love attachment is to a whole culture you've known intimately and in most cases happily, perhaps from childhood. And just like many cultures across the world, Mormon culture is religious. This means the social, historical, and ethical elements of the culture have been so intertwined with the religious belief system that it's all one seamless piece of fabric in the consciousness of its members. Growing up Mormon in a strongly Mormon community like Mesa, Arizona; Nauvoo, Illinois; or almost anyplace in Utah is like growing up Jewish in Tel Aviv or Brooklyn, Catholic in Florence, or Amish in Lancaster County, Pennsylvania.

Living in such communities means everything in life, from social activities in the marketplace to values and taboos to marriage patterns to church or worship practices, is religiously determined, altered, and maintained. So the bar mitzvah (or bat mitzvah) at age thirteen in a Jewish community becomes a rite of passage into adulthood as well as a religious ceremony, and the baptism at age eight in a Mormon community functions the same way and just as powerfully. Abstinence from eating pork and drinking alcohol in a Muslim community functions the same way as abstinence from alcohol, coffee, tea, and tobacco in a Mormon community. It's a health code that is at one and the same time a religious duty. The same shame and stigma will fall on the person who becomes a practicing homosexual in a Mormon community, in an Amish community, or in an Irish Catholic community, because in each of these social systems, the practice is seen as not only deviant but sinful, a social taboo that also violates God's moral order. Religion, ethics, social practices, family ties, even government—all are inextricably intertwined.

This intertwined reality forms and sustains the core cultural identity of the members of an ethnic community. The community becomes the place of our at-home-ness, our comfort zone, our "dignity, identity, security and continuity," as the Willowbank Report puts it.[1] An individual member's community becomes for him or her not just *a* people but *"my* people." Ruth the Moabitess, in converting to the Jewish faith, famously said to Naomi in one and the same breath, "Your people will be *my* people and your God *my* God" (Ruth 1:16, emphasis added). Similarly, Moses's famous words before Pharaoh, "Let *my* people go!" (Exod. 5:1, emphasis added), not only announced the demand of God but also proclaimed a choice Moses had made to throw in his lot with the Hebrews rather than the Egyptians. Clearly the intertwining of faith and community can be a good thing, as in the case of these biblical examples. Unfortunately, this intertwining force can also be perverted and turned to evil ends, as exemplified by various Islamic jihadist groups who carry out terrorist acts in the name of Allah.

What's important to notice here, though, is simply the profound connectedness of one's personal identity to the group's identity, the serious integration of "I" into "we." This connectedness explains why journeying out of the religion becomes so threatening, so painful, so fraught with difficulties: it isn't just a journey out of one's religious faith but also a journey out of one's *people*. Not just a change of belief system but also a change of loyalties occurs. Within the tight circle of family and community, when someone leaves, the rest might feel a sense of betrayal or forsakenness or repudiation. Sometimes members of the community feel the leaving as a rejection born of hatred, and sometimes they lash back, responding in kind to their perception. This decision is so much deeper, so much more than just choosing Pepsi over Coke!

For committed Mormons who leave, the force of this severance is filled with pain, as former Mormon Wayne

Jensen describes: "I know for a long, long time I was ex-
tremely tender. God broke my heart. Coming out of Mormonism is like going through a divorce and a funeral,
everything combined. It was just a devastating thing—but
He rebuilt me."[2]

Appreciation Campaign: The Good Things of Mormonism

We may also go further and begin to see the devastation
Wayne talks about as something with a deeper dimension:
what about all the good things of Mormonism one loses
when one leaves? Let's take a few pages to appreciate what
holds people in LDS faith and community. Remember, even
if we might classify some of the following items as merely
"perceived goods," they are real to the perceiver!

Family values. The LDS Church has certainly become
famous for its advocacy of strong and healthy family life.
One couple told me how they each grew up in a Mormon
home, became inactive in young adulthood, and then when
they had their first child became active again in the LDS
Church "to give a moral upbringing to our children just like
the one we got and appreciated." A woman friend of ours
said quite baldly, "I don't care about the doctrine. I joined
the Church because of its family values. You know, we're
really not all that different [from traditional Christians]
in our beliefs anyway." The value placed on marriage, on
family togetherness, on families united in church involvement, on religious training in the home—all this and more
is championed by the Mormon Church. In an age of family
disintegration, this emphasis feels reassuring and hopeful
for concerned parents.

Programs for all ages. The LDS Church has something
for everyone and extensive facilities for all these things
to take place in—large, beautiful gyms; dining facilities;
playgrounds; conference rooms; and more. A part of the

implementation of family values is church programs for children (called Primary) and young people (called Mutual) as well as for mothers and women in general (called Relief Society). Activities in these programs provide not only religious training and encouragement but also healthy alternatives to destructive lifestyles among peers; games, sports, dancing, and crafts are used to give the members outlets and social skills. Men have a program called Priesthood, which functions for male camaraderie and social development but also to advance men along the ladder of Eternal Progression and leadership roles in the church. There is even an alternative for singles, as pictured in the delightful, comedic LDS film *The Singles Ward* (see "Resources" at the end of the book), to give unmarried and divorced members a niche for social interaction and training—a clean alternative to the singles *bar*. Let's face it: leaving all this for the little Methodist church across town, which may not even have the resources for a youth group, can feel like quite a letdown.

A sense of community. Mormons shine at the intentionality and organization it takes to create a community. Wherever a critical mass of LDS people inhabits a local geographic area, they organize in neighborhood groupings called "wards." Where a critical mass does not exist in a small area, the ward may encompass a larger area like a town or section of a city, but the organized grouping will still be there, a localized community that takes its togetherness very seriously. The members of a ward, under the leadership of their bishop (the office roughly equivalent to "pastor"), hold religious services, do socials, organize vacation trips, visit each other at home (done mostly by "home teachers"), help package food for the LDS welfare system, run Boy Scout groups, and more. These extensive activities bond the members together and can meet the need for belonging that all humans have. In the ward, they call each other "brother" and "sister," an endearing practice that even spills over to "Gentiles" within ward boundaries.

Hazel and I are often addressed as "Brother Rowe" and
"Sister Rowe" by our neighbors, and it feels good because
it's quite a warm recognition.

I can attest to the power of these feelings of belonging,
which unsurprisingly becomes a power attracting and holding LDS people in the Mormon Church. This power occurs
on a more personal level, as illustrated by J. A. C. Redford,
with the practice of "blessing" he experienced at the hands
of his grandfather:

> Poppie blessed me many times in my life, not only at wa-
> tershed moments . . . but also when I was sick or needed
> strength to accomplish a difficult task. These blessings
> were a tangible expression of his love for me and a signifi-
> cant thread in the fabric of my life. These and other such
> experiences ultimately released forces that kept me in the
> Church long after my mind could no longer assent nor my
> heart believe.[3]

The ring of authority. If you're convinced there's only one
pipeline to God (to get the fullness of his truth) and your
church institution has exclusive rights to it, why would
you look elsewhere? This is effectively the claim of the LDS
Church, and for insiders it's a powerful one. The only prophets
who can speak as God's mouthpiece and the only apostles
who represent Jesus Christ, so the claim goes, are those who
hold the "priesthood authority" of the LDS Church. As mentioned before, "the heavens are open" is a compelling claim
and strictly attached to LDS leaders to make it reality: they
alone have the right to speak for God. Of course the conces-
sion "all religions have some truth" gets made regularly by
Mormon missionaries and friends, but the bottom-line belief
is that only the LDS Church has the fullness of truth, because
only it has the authority. "When the prophet speaks," a common saying goes, "the thinking has been done." For people
wanting a sense of certainty, reassurance, and undoubting
faith, this becomes quite appealing.

"A demanding religion." Perhaps at first blush it sounds strange and a bit austere for LDS President Gordon B. Hinckley to say, "We have a demanding religion and that is one of the things that attracts people to this church."[4] In addition to the three-hour Sunday service-and-teaching time in your ward, as a Latter-day Saint you would face Fast Sunday once each month (foregoing two meals and giving the food expense to the poor), personal and family scripture studies and prayers daily, Family Home Evening each Monday, perhaps Boy Scouts, youth program, giving or receiving "home teaching," the bishop's "calling" to you for service in a specific position in the ward, a two-year mission if you're between nineteen and twenty-one, genealogical research and journaling on your family records, baptisms for the dead and other temple rites (assuming you've worked righteously enough to become "temple worthy," as discussed above), and many more items that could be added. This imposing list may sound exhausting, but it's also specific, clearly defined, and challenging. It appeals because it gives clear roles and expectations and a chance to rise to the challenge and make some constructive contribution of one's life, especially if following it is seen as following the divine will.

Health and wealth. One university student I met was a self-confessed alcoholic with little religious background and lots of desperation over his addiction. He was contacted by Mormon missionaries working on campus who told him about the Word of Wisdom—the Mormons' sacred health code forbidding alcohol and other harmful substances—and also told stories about LDS people getting delivered from their alcoholism. He was immediately impressed, even astonished over the professed track record of this major institution: ten million people with no alcohol usage! Certain this "positive peer group of millions" was the cure for his problem, he joined the LDS Church almost immediately (despite my best efforts to dissuade him). Granted, his picture of the LDS Church was a bit romanticized, but still, the commitment to these kinds of health practices becomes very attractive to some people. The same power to attract is true of the entrepreneurial, industrious impulses of Mormon community, which has generated great wealth among some members. People admire financial LDS success models such as the Marriott family, philanthropist John Huntsman, and Larry Miller (owner of the Utah Jazz basketball team); for many it is hard not to make the underlying assumption that their success is attributable to their faithfulness as Mormons. Also, the practice of tithing generates great income for Church programs and facilities—for example, the very generous LDS Church welfare system is applauded by Mormons and non-Mormons alike.

Experiential "truth." A very standard, bottom-line reason many, many Mormons join and remain in the LDS Church is they "have a testimony." This usually means that a dramatic or heartfelt experience has occurred to them confirming "the truth" of Mormonism, and the experience gets labeled and reinforced by the LDS community as a "testimony"—a message from God. One young man told me he had longed for years to find in his Protestant church an experience of "truth," but it would come to him only in tiny "particles in the air" now and then during a church service. He would sense them as little bits of goodness, which he'd try to reach out and grab with his spirit, but they never satisfied because they were too few and far between. Then one day he visited a Mormon church service, and "the air was thick with these truth-particles! I've simply never been the same." Mystical, feeling-based experiences like this—often when reading the Book of Mormon—get affirmed in testimony meetings and have a powerful grip on members who have confidence in them.

The cradle of familiarity. If you were reared from infancy in a faithful Mormon household, Mormonism may have become the air you breathe, the ropes you know, and the cultural comfort zone where you're at home. If your life continues on basically happy, undisturbed, and agreeable, you may simply figure this is as good as it gets from womb to tomb. Of course, this happens with every religious group. Some members remain unreflective and lukewarm; they are the masses who never question the basic assumed rightness and normalcy of their religion. What holds them in the group has less to do with commitment than with inertia. The beliefs and values seem sensible enough, the lifeways are familiar, the support system intact. Why bother changing?

That last question, frankly, remains at issue for any of the good things of Mormonism one experiences and enjoys, and there may be more than the ones listed here.

So If It's That Good, Why Change?

Well, why *do* some LDS folk—despite these numerous appealing aspects of the Mormon Church—have a change of heart and mind and end up risking the journey out? To focus the question, let's first recognize that not all journeys out take the same shape. As mentioned earlier, some former Mormons are on a spiritual quest and journey into another religious option (Buddhist, Muslim, Hindu, Christian, whatever), and some simply go secular. Often this latter type simply becomes a lapsed member who is on the LDS Church rolls but no longer practices the religion. Such members are referred to among Mormons as "inactive" or, to use the slang term, "Jack Mormons," and many times these people remain Mormon culturally but not religiously (Mormon in name and ethnic identity, but not in religious practice).

Wherever they are on the spectrum between the religious and the secular, however, these transitioning Mormons tend to be motivated by one or more of three general patterns of response to the question, "Why change?"

One motive is *hunger for God*. This implies, of course, an unfulfilled longing for a kind of deity the person did not discover in Mormonism and for a personal connection to that deity. Let's look at these two aspects of the hunger a little more closely.

Sometimes when LDS people get exposed to the wider world out there and begin to appreciate beyond the straw-figure level other notions of God that are possible outside Mormonism, they get intrigued. If they move in the direction of historic, traditional Christian theology, they bump into a God who is originary (the classic uncaused Cause, or uncreated Creator), changeless, transcendent of our human nature (honestly "Other"), and truly supreme, not to mention triune. This kind of being cannot fit into the categories of Mormon theology because this is not a God we could become like, no matter how many "eternities" we had to spend on the project! He is not just one of the beings caught in a cosmic "Eternal Progression round" alongside innumerable others working their way up the ladder; he is truly supreme *over* the cosmos. He is not derived from anything or anyone else. Perhaps in a sense more intuitive than verbalized, these LDS travelers have realized that a god who is merely an "exalted man" can be *admired* with respect, honor, and soberness, but he cannot be *worshipped*; that is, nothing about him stirs the sense of unmitigated awe that would properly be accorded to a majestically transcendent, sovereign Other such as orthodox Christian theology presents. These travelers hunger for a God this big.

But they don't just want him on paper; they don't just want him in the niceties of theoretical abstraction. They want to *know him*! They want to *personally* connect. In the middle of their sincere and abundant religious activity—all those meetings, tithings, and temple works, which constitute the primary way their hunger for God manifests itself—these Mormons sense there's something missing. This something, though hard to name for many of them, can be conceived as a personal relationship with a God who is truly transcendent and majestic but knows your name, knows *you* as a friend. One former Mormon told me of a time in his life, shortly after his mission, when the LDS Institute of Religion at his college held a class on "comparative religions." In the final session, he said, some guests from various Christian churches were present, and one Protestant guy was asked to pray. The former Mormon I refer to remembers this as a turning point in his life, simply because the way this Christian prayed was so intensely personal. Unlike his experience with Mormon prayers (including his own), this one was not distant, monotone, and "Thee-and-Thou" formal but warm, conversational, "Dear-Daddy" intimate, as a friend talks to a friend, and yet it had lost nothing in reverential awe and honor. He said to himself immediately, "*That's* the personal connection I'm looking for." He kept looking, and today he's a joyfully committed traditional Christian.

A second motive for changing is *deal-breaking inconsistencies*. Basically, these become foci for cognitive dissonance or heartbreaking disappointment. They may be doctrinal, ethical, or a mixture of the two. Some transitioners get disturbed by the limits of a god who is subject to laws he didn't make or who before 1978 disallowed black men from entering the LDS priesthood and will apparently never let women join it. Some are disturbed by recent studies of the DNA of Native Americans that make it impossible for them to be what the Book of Mormon claims they are—Jewish. Some are disturbed by a Mormon teaching that doesn't square with what's clearly in the Bible (e.g., Jesus Christ and Lucifer being "spirit brothers"). Some look at LDS history and find incidents that seem to fly in the face of the church's own proclaimed standards. Some encounter what they consider egregious ethical inconsistencies at a more personal level—for example, a molestation of one's daughter by "brother so-and-so" down the street, or a divorce by an upstanding Mormon wife after the husband and father had "done everything right according to the Church." Both examples in the previous sentence are real-life incidents reported to me as justification for the victims falling away from the LDS Church. Such ruptures in one's trust can be a final straw for some people.

The third motive is *besetting burdens*. Many, like J. A. C. Redford testifies, find themselves hopelessly weighed down by the shame and guilt of failure to keep up with the commandments and other duties:

> There were steps, there were lists, there were things that had to be done, there were commandments to be obeyed. These multiplied over the years from the time you were a young boy to the time you are in your mid-twenties to late twenties working within the systems of the church trying to serve, doing all the things you are supposed to do—doing your home teachings, conducting your personal priesthood interviews, etc. There are a billion things you end up having to be responsible for. And I was just feeling like I was falling short. "I am not making it, I am not able to do these things." I knew I needed salvation when I came to terms with that, when I didn't let myself off the hook or rationalize it. I knew I needed redemption and it had to come from outside of myself. There was nothing I could do to fix it. That is when the grace of God really took on power. . . . My own sin got the better of me and I needed God to rescue me. . . . And He did![5]

Sometimes it's a more personal issue of guilt over a sin pattern one cannot conquer, like greed or alcoholism or porn addiction, and the transitioner cannot seem to find resources enough in the Mormon Church to overcome this captivity, to slay the inner giant. Persons may, if they do not simply give themselves over to what weighs their conscience down, move out of Mormonism in their quest for a cure.

In summary, we who would find openings for the gospel of the Bible into the lives of Mormon people need first to become aware of what truly motivates them. Remembering they are individuals and each has his or her own story, they may hold any of a number of reasons they were attracted to the LDS Church and continue to find that attraction valid. Because of the "goods" the LDS Church produces and the intertwined community of Mormon people (faith and cultural values being inextricably wound together), it can be difficult and even painful to journey out. Yet our Mormon friends experience tensions and other difficulties, which lead some to take this journey despite its hardships. In the next chapter, we'll look more closely at two stories of people who have dealt with these tensions, seeing what lessons we can extract to help us.

For Discussion and More

1. What factors can create travail for Mormons who take the journey out? Can you relate anything in your own life to the reality of tearing apart from an "intertwined community"?
2. Evaluate the pros and cons of living in an "intertwined community." Notice how it works in the biblical account of Israel and the historic church. Then, using that template, try to discern how it works in Mormonism from any information or experience you have. Where have they "got it right," and where have they got it dysfunctional?
3. Try to procure a copy of the Mormon-produced film *Brigham City*. After viewing it, discuss the characters and the kind of community life portrayed: where is it real, and where is it glossy? Notice especially the final "Sacrament Meeting" scene, and discuss what it might mean in light of the story and especially in light of LDS beliefs and values.
4. Of the "goods" Mormonism delivers (the ones named in this chapter, and there may be more besides), pick any three and discuss what it might take to give them up and what would take their place for a for-

mer Mormon who had done so and then joined *your* church.

5. Interview an LDS person, and ask what he or she finds attractive in the Mormon Church. Alternatively, ask a former LDS person what was attractive about the Mormon Church as well as what problem or "deal breaker" compelled him or her to leave. Discuss the responses in terms of what will help you relate to LDS people for the sake of the gospel.

7

Love It or Leave It

Two Stories

Some stay, some leave. Many of the faithful honestly love the LDS Church and could not imagine leaving it. In fact, as a general rule, Mormons do not easily leave their church and its culture even if they want to. Many elect to "grin and bear it" as insiders even when they may experience great tensions and problems due to their church's demands. Of course, this implies they still love it too much to leave it, that is, love it more than the alternative, regardless of the pains and problems. Rarely does the outside world (especially in their ward) see any problem, because nothing shows behind the grin, even if they are being torn to pieces inside.

"God Bless You Please, Mrs. Robinson"

Mrs. Janet Robinson, faithful LDS wife of a professor at Brigham Young University, allows us a glimpse behind the grin. We'll start by looking at her story, a love-it-and-stay story, before considering the story of a couple who left. Dr. Stephen Robinson put the account of his wife's travail in print in his book *Believing Christ*.[1] Hers is a case study in the quiet desperation some experience due to the effects of a core motive of Mormon culture, namely, the notion of "conditional grace." Let's see what we can learn from her, and from her husband's response, which well represents the response of the LDS Church.

After many years of consistent living in compliance with the Mormon religion, Janet came to a point of crisis within herself. It appears, from the testimony her husband gives of the "sudden change," that she became numb and entered a kind of spiritual coma. He puts it this way: "One day the lights just went out. It was as though Janet had died to spiritual things; she had burned out. She became very passive in her attitude toward the Church."

What horrified Stephen most of all, though, was the sheer, threatening interiority of his wife's behavior, which left him totally shut out because "she wouldn't talk about it; she wouldn't tell me what was wrong." This sort of silent treatment can drive a husband crazy, of course, and that's exactly what happened. For nearly two weeks he needled and nagged, pried and pressured to get something out of her, until one night she exploded:

All right. Do you want to know what's wrong? I'll tell you what's wrong—I can't do it anymore. I can't lift it. My load is just too heavy. I can't do all the things I'm supposed to. I can't get up at 5:30, and bake bread, and sew clothes, and help the kids with their homework, and do my own homework, and make their lunches, and do the housework, and do my Relief Society stuff, and have scripture study, and do my genealogy, and write my congressman, and go to PTA meetings, and get our year's supply organized, and go to my stake meetings, and write the missionaries. . . .

You may recall J. A. C. Redford's comment in the last chapter about how a Mormon child grows into adulthood with "steps . . . lists . . . things that had to be done . . . commandments to be obeyed," which "multiplied over the years" until before he's thirty there are "a billion things you end up having to be responsible for." One observation here should be clear: this unrelenting pressure, this heaviness of work obligation in Mormon experience, disregards gender. No one who seeks to be truly faithful gets left out.

To me, a startling and unusually revealing piece of Stephen Robinson's description of this night, which he says was "one of the longest nights of our life together," occurs in these words of his: "She just started naming, one after the other, all the things she couldn't do or couldn't do perfectly—all the individual bricks that had been laid on her back in the name of perfection until they had crushed the light out of her." Frankly, if you're like me, you'll find yourself aching inside for both of them when you read words like these. What catches my attention is not only the vividness of Stephen's metaphor, "bricks . . . laid on her back," but also the references, twice in one sentence, to an expectation to be perfect—the real cause of all the heaviness of her load. These bricks had been "laid on her back *in the name of perfection.*"

We can immediately see the outworking in human experience of the core Mormon doctrine we studied earlier: "Eternal Progression" gets played out as an expectation to live as "gods in embryo," that is, to live perfectly! In Mormon belief, this is part of what Jesus meant when he said, "Be ye therefore perfect, even as your Father which is in heaven is perfect" (Matt. 5:48 KJV). The consequent toll it took on Janet is what makes me ache most as I empathize (and believe me, I really do) with her loving husband having to watch the brightness vanish from her eyes and the zest vanish from her life as these "bricks . . . crushed the light out of her."

And that was just the *beginning* of the Robinsons' long night. Janet continued her venting:

> I try not to yell at the kids . . . but I can't seem to help it; I get mad, and I yell. So then I try not to get mad, but I eventually do. I try not to have hard feelings toward this person and that person, but I do. I'm just not very Christ-like. No matter how hard I try to love everyone, I fail. I don't have the talent Sister X has, and I'm just not as sweet as Sister Y. Steve, I'm just not perfect—I'm never going to be perfect, and I just can't pretend anymore that I am. I've finally admitted to myself that I can't make it to the Celestial Kingdom, so why should I break my back trying?

She puts an even finer point on her distress over failing the religious-perfection project with the words, "I'm never going to be perfect, and I just can't pretend anymore that I am." *There's* the rub! As if expecting oneself to be perfect isn't crippling enough, she bears the additional burden of *pretending* to be perfect! Here the intertwined nature of Mormon community functions at its most powerful: the pressure is not only internal but external, not only private but public, for one must not only *try* to be obedient (perfectly obedient), but even when failing one must *look like* one is succeeding. I must say I'm flatly amazed Stephen and Janet went into print with such vulnerable confession as we read here, and I very much respect them for taking the risk. Janet even presses her admission of weakness and failure to the ultimate level by conceding she "can't make it to the Celestial Kingdom."

Let me recount here a direct experience Hazel and I had with some friends. One Friday afternoon, Brenda Lindquist (let's call her) knocked on our door. She and her husband, "Steve," nearby and very devout Mormon neighbors, asked us to feed their dog for the weekend while they were away on a trip. We agreed and went over moments later to learn the how-tos and get the house key from them. As we turned to

leave, Brenda nervously spoke up with a request and statement I can only describe as heartrending. We could tell they
felt at risk, and yet somehow safe, with us. "Steve and I have
to take our son to a detox clinic in California. He's become
a severe alcoholic. We know you two are close to Christ and
want to ask you to pray for us, please." Then came haunting,
poignant words Hazel and I will never forget: "We haven't
told anyone in the ward about this." All that community,
all that brothering and sistering they had, and yet when
the real test of love came, here they were turning to their
non-Mormon, Christian neighbors! In that moment I got a
vivid picture of what tremendous pressure our dear Mormon
friends must be under as they pretend at perfection.

That's where Janet Robinson found herself as well. The
final salvo in her rant occurs in the following dialogue,
recounted by her husband:

> I asked Janet, "Do you have a testimony?" She responded,
> "Of course I do—that's what's so terrible. I know the gospel
> is true, I just can't live up to it." I asked her if she had kept
> her baptismal covenants, and she replied, "No. I've tried
> and I've tried, but I can't keep all the commandments all
> the time." I asked her if she had kept the covenants she
> had made in the temple, and again she said, "I try, but
> no matter how hard I try, I don't seem to be able to do all
> that's asked of me."

It's hard to miss the exasperation in her comments. How
much covenant keeping is enough? How close to perfection
does one's obedience need to be? How perfect is "perfect,"
anyway? Now, let's be honest: many traditional Christians,
forgetting God's grace in everyday life, put themselves under
the same burden—especially if they're perfectionists (like
myself)—by personality and cultural conditioning. The
difference is that in standard Mormonism and in Mormon
culture this expectation of perfection is institutionalized
and official; such is not the case in biblical Christianity.

Stephen believes he can help his wife. As he describes his response to her, we get a good sense of the classic Mormon answer to this kind of spiritual burnout. He diagnoses the problem as a failure on Janet's part to fully grasp not only the demands of the gospel but also "the core of the gospel—the atonement of Christ." Here we encounter Dr. Robinson's effort to explain the LDS understanding of the relationship between grace and works, and he does it by way of a parable from family life. Once his daughter wanted to buy a bicycle, but it was far too pricey for her to afford. He had told his daughter that if she diligently saved all the money she could and put it toward the purchase, he would pay the rest. In other words, *if* she did all she could do, he would do what she couldn't do. Similarly, the Mormon "gospel" claims Christ's atonement covers what we can't *if* we cover what we can. The "what we can" part means, in Mormon spirituality, trying to keep all the commandments as much as possible and with a good attitude. The classic LDS support for this view comes from the Book of Mormon statement, "It is by grace that we are saved, after all we can do" (II Nephi 25:23). Stephen's bicycle parable pictures for us very well what the Mormon understanding is: if we want to progress to our goal in the Eternal Progression plan (buy the bicycle), we must give all we have with a good attitude (pay all we possibly can) in order to qualify for the help—or "grace"—Jesus offers (the balance, which he'll pay).

This give-your-all-to-get-God's-grace message really amounts to a "gospel" of *conditional grace*. God's grace in Jesus Christ only comes to us on the condition that we try our hardest. In the end, this "gospel" makes God's acceptance contingent on our performance. While it may sound nice and comforting up front and on the surface, it simply boils down to another performance-driven system. Frankly, while promising Janet the moon (or at least a shiny new bicycle), it only delivers more bricks to her back! At best, it's very difficult for me to believe this message truly satisfied her.

Janet Robinson, of course, was hungering for the same thing we all need, namely, acceptance from God that is completely independent of our performance, traditionally understood as God's unmerited favor in Jesus Christ toward sinners. That is the *real* grace the Bible talks about, which is utterly unconditional, undeserved, and unexpected yet actually motivates and energizes people to pour out their lives in sheer gratitude, doing the good works God calls for and for which we are made (Luke 15; Eph. 2:8–10). It's truly "amazing"!

Grace on Grace: The Murphys' Story

Such is the grace Paul and Jenna Murphy found, or better, the grace that found them. I'm privileged to know this couple because we belong to the same church community. Here's their story.

Both grew up LDS, though Paul's parents remained devout while Jenna's became inactive, or "Jack Mormon," during her later childhood. Both were taken to church meetings regularly as young children. Both of them feel quite appreciative of their Mormon upbringing with its positive values, religious awareness, and moral grounding. Paul flatly states, "I *loved* growing up LDS! I wanted to be a defender of the faith!" Still, they've journeyed out of the LDS Church for reasons we'll explore. God has innumerable tricks up his sleeve for getting through to each human being about his desire to have a personal relationship with him or her. In Jenna's case, siblings seemed to play a primary role; in Paul's, it was more like a haunting presence from the Bible that bled its way through the filter of Mormon culture and right into his soul.

Two of Jenna's three older siblings left the nest for college. While the two were there, first her brother and then her sister became something called "born-again Christians." This mystified the family a bit, and Jenna herself had no idea what to make of it until her born-again older sister took her to a Christian camp when she was thirteen. There Jenna understood this thing about a personal, saving relationship with God through Jesus Christ, and though it was rudimentary, she "accepted Christ." But after camp she went back home to her Mormon household and network of friends and church activities. By college she was disinterested in the LDS religion (or any other) and ran away from everything her household represented, experimenting with the party life. Something was haunting her inside, and her born-again brother tried to "rescue" her, but she repressed it all. She dated and married Paul during those years.

Paul had known Jenna in high school; now he was a noteworthy, respected "RM" (returned missionary), ready to settle down—a prize catch! However, he'd been haunted for several years by a very specific and central Scripture in his life, John 17:3: "And this is life eternal, that they might know thee the only true God, and Jesus Christ, whom thou hast sent" (as he would recall it from the King James Version, which is what all Mormons use). Frequently and fervently he had prayed these words: "Jesus, I want to know you." He read through Mormon writer James Talmadge's book, well regarded by LDS people, *Jesus the Christ*, and from it Paul got what he still considers a basically good picture of Christ, which stirred his passion even more to really know this person. But a true personal relationship with Jesus, a friend-to-friend relationship, eluded him. He saw it and tasted it only vicariously through others who claimed they really did know Jesus and acted in ways true to that claim, which invariably shocked him and left him responding, *"That's* it, *that's* what I'm after!"

All this was going on inside Paul when he and Jenna married. But they stayed in the familiar world and culture of the Mormon Church, and when their first child was born, they agreed to become active again so the kids would have a "moral foundation" and the family could be united. They tried it for a while but found they had changed enough to feel out of sync with some of the things happening in LDS meetings and services. For example, they both had some issues about the role of women and African-Americans in Mormonism, and they (especially Paul) noticed the conspicuous absence of Jesus being regarded as preeminent in actual practice. And besides, where was that *personal* connection to Jesus Christ for which they hungered?

A friend Paul had known as a neighbor since childhood invited him to Bible Study Fellowship, an offer he was ready to accept. In seriously trekking through the world of the Bible, Paul encountered Jesus again and again and again. It became clear what he had to do to fulfill the longstanding desire of his heart that had been named by John 17:3. One night as he was driving to BSF, he simply and guilelessly prayed to Jesus, saying, "My life is yours," and asking to be born again. He was, and everything began to change. Around the same time, Jenna, who was making the same discoveries as Paul in searching the biblical story, likewise gave her life to Christ unreservedly. Shortly after, they became involved in our church. They have become excited, visionary youth leaders and true, impassioned worshippers of the Jesus whom they now at last know as not only "the Lord" but *their* Lord, not only "the Savior" but *their* Savior, not only "the friend of sinners" but *their* friend.

To cap off the Murphys' story about making the transition from Mormonism into traditional Christianity, we must pay special attention to the importance of relating *personally* to God through Jesus Christ. This and nothing else is the resolving chord in their song and the bottom line they proclaim to others. They especially love to proclaim it to their LDS family and friends, and even missionaries, and in appendix 3 you can look more closely at how they go about it. For now, suffice it to say they stress two sensibilities in telling their story: (1) they have virtually no bad things to say about the LDS Church (in fact, both Paul and Jenna speak of it in very appreciative terms); and (2) they simply say they never found Jesus Christ in the

LDS Church, that is, never found a *personal* relationship
with him there.

Conclusions: Learning, Loving, and Leaving

"Love it or leave it" may ring a bit simplistic, it turns out,
for the real situation of Mormons in transition. The story
of Janet Robinson reminds us that some LDS people may
not love the LDS Church and its "gospel," at least not *all*
the time, and yet cannot see any viable scenario in which
they would find it thinkable to leave. So entrenched are
they, and so attached to the core convictions and cultural
values of Mormonism (e.g., it's the "one true Church" and
the place of all family and friends), leaving simply never
becomes an option, *no matter what*. By the time one has
the status and influence of a high-profile, popular, widely
published Brigham Young University professor, this may
be the case regardless of how many bricks are on your
wife's back—or yours.

The Murphys, on the other hand, found it not only thinkable but necessary to leave, yet it's not at all fair to them
to say they stopped loving the LDS Church. In some ways,
they left but still love it in terms of core values (industry,
cooperation, community service), cultural lifeways (emphasis on the family and clean health practices), and certainly its people. It's plain to see that the Murphys love and
truly respect Mormon people, including family, neighbors,
friends, co-workers, missionaries, whomever. At the same
time, it's also true they found a higher, more captivating,
and life-determining love that drew them eventually into
their journey out of the Mormon Church, namely, their
intimate, heartfelt love of Jesus Christ as a person.

What else can we learn from these two stories as we
consider implications for our understanding of Mormon
people in order to faithfully and compassionately bring
the Bible's Good News into their lives? I can see at least

six lessons here. Maybe you can see even more, but let's start with this grab bag of observations (in no particular order).

1. *Relax and be hopeful! God is already working in the lives of your LDS friends and family—trust him and join him.* Whether the Lord brings into one's life a crisis of legalistic overload and failure to "lift it" as with Janet Robinson, or a deep hunger to know Christ personally as with Paul Murphy, or a gentle rescue operation by the Hound of Heaven as with Jenna Murphy, or something else, it is our Redeemer Lord who is at work. These events and experiences are not accidents but are "determined" by God "so that men would seek him and perhaps reach out for him and find him" (Acts 17:26–27). Let's carefully observe what particular way God seems to be at work in a person's life and think that way as we relate to him or her.

2. *Appreciation of Mormon culture works wonders.* It opens doors into the lives of our friends, averts defenses before they are raised, and often even heightens curiosity about why (if there's so much to appreciate) one is *not* LDS. This dynamic is especially true and compelling for former Mormons, like the Murphys, when they express appreciation of good Mormon values and practices. But anyone can cultivate this practice, and there are at least two corollaries to the principle that indicate why we can genuinely express appreciation. First, the LDS cultural filter can allow people to see the real Jesus and move toward him—yes, even despite some unorthodox, unbiblical teachings about Christ—just as happened to Paul. Second, we can learn some things from Mormons—about community, about serving people, about organizing for mission work—and not as a mere ploy to "get them to hear us out" but for our benefit as well as to truly understand and relate to them.

3. *"Conditional grace" drives Mormon experience and sometimes drives a Mormon right out of the LDS Church!*

The "Mrs. Robinsons" of the LDS world will need to find
various coping devices to carry their load and keep going
even though the bricks "crush the light out of" them.
Others will sometimes cave in, then look for alternatives.
And the more seriously conscientious Mormon people
are about practicing their religion with all its demands,
the more extreme the weight they will feel and the more
at-risk for a crisis they will become. The Janet Robinson story displays this. Remember, as Janet said and the
anecdote about the Lindquists reinforces, if one can't
be perfect in keeping the LDS requirements, one must
nevertheless *look* perfect, a double-pressure pretending
act Janet and others experience. We can offer them a
glorious balm—the experience of unconditional, amazing grace. Indeed, this may be the greatest and most important thing we have and they lack. We may become a
shelter of hope and trust for LDS people caught in this
double bind. We'll find that real grace invariably becomes
a stunningly beautiful thing to LDS people who have little
to no taste of it in their previous experience.

4. *If we traditional Christians are seen merely to operate
with a "Christian" version of the perfectionist's "gospel,"
we frankly have nothing to say to Mormons.* Here we have
a kind of counterpart to the point above. Clearly, if our
Mormon friends see us enslaved to a set of rules to vali-
date our relationship with God and others, they'll end
up thinking "what's the difference?"—and rightly so. If
they see us busily dressing up our image to look "pure"
by compliance with rules about what to drink, what to
wear, what meetings to attend, what movies and TV shows
not to watch, well, all our God talk about "grace" will
ring hollow.

5. *To leave the LDS fold, one must either come to love an
alternative much more than one loves the LDS Church or
must come to experience serious doubt or disaffection.* For
the Murphys, the powerful magnet of a real and personal
relationship with the real and personal Jesus pulled them

away from the Mormon Church. They couldn't find this relationship inside the Church, so they had to go outside it. Others who transition out get disaffected or begin to doubt the claims and practices of the Church, like criteria for "worthiness," pressures on women (like Janet Robinson describes), marginalized treatment of divorced members, dearth of archaeology and history supporting the Book of Mormon story, and many other issues.

6. *For those Mormons who "love it and stay," the normal and ultimate trump card is "having a testimony."* That's why Stephen Robinson goes straight to this question as the core issue when he talks to his distraught wife: "Do you have a testimony?" This must be established before all else because it determines the validity of the LDS Church's claim to be the "one true Church" (in Mormon understanding). And on the personal level, it gets valorized by the culture in a way that gives one an unassailable reason to stay in the Mormon Church.

This final point takes us to the next step in our exploration of Mormon culture. At the root of any issue about the LDS Church that may cause a member to take the journey out is a much deeper issue. It's an issue every one of us must resolve in some way in our quest to know our Creator. We may describe it this way: how do we come to know what is actually the revealed truth of God? This profound question, this issue, really is the crux of the matter and the apex of our ascent in this book's journey into Mormon culture. We're now ready to discuss it in our next chapter.

For Discussion and More

1. See if you can explain or give some reasons why Mormons who stay in the LDS Church despite pain and major problems "love it more than the alternative." What might some of the alternatives be?

2. What does Stephen Robinson mean when he says about Janet's crisis that she started naming "all the individual bricks that had been laid on her back in the name of perfection"? Can you name what some of those bricks would be? To what does "in the name of perfection" refer?

3. Define and give an image of the LDS notion of "conditional grace." Do you think traditional Christians may sometimes and in some circles practice a form of "conditional grace"? What's the solution to this problem, and how can Christians humbly and empathetically discuss it with their Mormon friends?

4. What was the deepest hunger the Murphys had that, at least in their experience, could not be fulfilled from inside the LDS Church? How might their story help you deal understandingly with Mormons you know or meet?

5. Respond to this statement from Dallas Willard about a traditional Christian understanding of grace and works: "Grace is not opposed to *effort*: grace is opposed to *earning*."[2] Can you explain clearly how we Christians are committed to a life of good works and yet believe we are saved, as some put it, by grace alone through faith alone in Christ alone?

8

The Heart of the Matter

Learning to Speak "Mormonese"

Penelope J. Stokes delightfully recounts through her historical fiction the events of the Christmas story, the story of "enfleshing the holy in human form." Her chapter about the angel visiting "a bunch of dirty shepherds, outcasts" tells of a shepherd named Jonathan who reports to Mary what he had seen and heard. Here's part of the dialogue:

> "The angel said there would be peace to those who have found favor with God. But I don't know if that includes us. I mean, I've never been very religious—"
> "Maybe religion has little to do with God's favor," Mary suggested. "What does your heart tell you? Is your soul at peace?"[1]

The Ache of the Ungraced Heart

Rather ironically, those who *are* "very religious" very often find their souls no more at peace than those who aren't. In fact, persons of sensitivity and keenly sharpened conscience who are also "very religious" will usually be much less at peace than others. After all their strivings, their hearts still condemn them with a feeling of nagging not-good-enoughness that says, "You don't yet measure up." This predicament applies especially to those involved in high-demand religions such as Mormonism, and most especially if they are conscientious about the practice of their faith. For such people, the unconditional, undeserved, unexpected favor of God (his "amazing grace"), which truly and finally "fixes it" and sets one's soul at peace, *has to* come off like some angelic message, *has to* sound like good news!

Or does it?

Strange as it may seem, this message—as we traditional Christians often present it—may not always sound so good to the ears of our LDS friends. How can this be, and how can we do better? This chapter, which is really the crescendo of our entire song in this book, explores the obstacles and opportunities of proclaiming the Good News to our Mormon friends *in a way that really sounds like good news to them!*

Why We Must Speak "Mormonese"

We're interested, then, in learning to share the gospel so it becomes meaningful, compelling, and attractive within the LDS cultural frame. This entails our extending to Mormons not only the attitude of divine grace but also the articulation of that grace, which results from our learning to speak "Mormonese"—the language of experience.

We'll reflect on what that looks like in the next chapter, but first we must understand just why it's worth our effort to learn this language. Here we need to borrow a term from the discourse of philosophy to give a name to the final piece of LDS worldview that we must understand in order to communicate successfully with our Mormon friends. It's the term *epistemology*, which simply refers to the study of how we know what we take to be true. At first blush this term, this concept, may seem a bit obtusely academic, but epistemology stands right at the center of our evangelism issues with LDS people.

All people and all cultures operate with some sort of epistemology, some way of knowing what they consider true about the world we live in. And the sorts run a wide gamut. So, for example, social systems or ethnic groups in modern, secular, scientific, technologically "civilized" societies (the dominant cultural ethos in places like North America, Japan, France, and Germany) tend to operate with an *epistemology of scientific rationalism*: the cultural "we" know something to be true because nine out of ten doctors say so, or it can be "proved" in a test tube, or the scientific community of "experts" has declared it true. Such declarations are based on scientists' findings from the use of rigorous empirical research methods and scientific tools such as microscopes, telescopes, satellites, and ultrasound machines. The trusted, culturally validated way of knowing in most of the West, then, boils down to this: good scientific method used by "experts" produces reliable, accurate, true knowledge of the world we live in.

Both pros and cons result from this epistemological base, but it is nevertheless the way of knowing that most modern folk in these societies have trusted (notwithstanding current critiques and changes). So, while the scientifically known structure of the atom and of DNA molecules can explain a lot about what is true of the world we live in—even revealing the legal guilt or innocence of death-row criminal suspects through DNA "fingerprinting"—this way of knowing also has built-in risks and limits. At this writing, humanity deals with gnarly ethical issues surrounding human cloning efforts and sophisticated weapons of mass destruction. Many wonder if scientific research has not opened a Pandora's box and led humans down the path of playing God.

Other large questions also arise as we critique this epistemology of scientific rationalism. Is the natural universe of physics and biological data really "all there is, all there ever was, and all there ever will be," as the brilliant scientific philosopher Carl Sagan famously claimed on his PBS series *Cosmos*? Can DNA mapping ever show a graph of the motives in a human being's heart? Will there ever be a telescope powerful enough to see heaven or hell or the New Jerusalem? Where is the satellite technology that can spot the geographic locations of demon activity on the earth?

Questions like these may trouble us enough to consider the potential of other ways of knowing. A different, more "primitive" sort of social system, rooted, say, in a *spiritual narrative epistemology*, assumes a tribally owned, grand story that tells us what is true of the world and how we fit into it. This epistemological way would assume the scientific, rationalist way of knowing is myopic and cannot tell the whole truth—maybe not even the most important truth—about the real world. Cultures like this are quite common in vast places on earth, such as much of the African continent, the Pacific Islands, and Latin America. These cultures do not believe the only way of knowing is through scientific instruments and methods. They believe an individual's experience and tribal storytelling that reports the group's experiences give access to unseen, spiritual realities as well. Thus, encounters with angels and demons and divine healings and curses and prophecies and testings of the heart are normal aspects of what such cultures come to know as true and real. Again, these aspects cannot be found through test tubes and telescopes, so the means of knowing them is spiritual and experiential.

Christians and others whose worldview includes a spiritual realm may appreciate this kind of cultural frame and even see its epistemology as something similar to what is obtained in the historical context of the life of Jesus. After all, from the turning of water into wine to the casting out of demons, walking on the top of the sea to raising Lazarus from death, there are certainly plenty of angels and demons and spiritual power encounters popping up in the narrative of the Bible and messing with the material realm! Serious traditional Christians take these events not as legend or religious fairy tale but as real, material history.

Epistemologies, then, differ across a spectrum with many shades in between these two models, making it patently clear that not everybody comes to know what is regarded as true in the same way.

LDS Epistemology: Knowing by Heart

Now, what does all this have to do with bridging into the world of our Mormon friends for the sake of the gospel? When we consider Mormon epistemology, we find ourselves drawn into a cultural frame more like the second model (spiritual narrative) than the first (scientific rationalism). Let's be careful to observe, though, that this does not mean LDS people have no trust in scientific methods or technological tools to determine some aspects of truth. An American Mormon couple will believe the ultrasound report on the sex of their unborn baby just as readily as any other American couple. But between these physical, material realities and the more spiritual realities, the common LDS worldview makes a radical bifurcation, a division of two kinds of reality into very distinct, hermetically sealed compartments, and the epistemologies to access these two are likewise radically distinct.

So in the Mormon cultural frame, the way of knowing spiritual realities, spiritual truth, is through what we might

best label *an epistemology of romanticism*. Simply put,
what Mormons are taught to trust as the way of knowing
spiritual truth is their experienced feelings.

More specifically, in the highly religious culture of Mormonism, the ultimate test for knowing truth about the
world and divine involvement with it is a "burning in the
bosom"—a deep feeling one experiences, known as a "testimony." Initially this is used as the test for knowing that the
Book of Mormon is true revelation from God, but it doesn't
stop there. This emphasis on feelings as the way of knowing spiritual truth, this romantic epistemology, fills every
corner of Mormon life, discourse, and social interaction. It
extends from private spiritual experiences to weekly church
meetings and more. For example, in Sacrament meetings
or Fast and Testimony meetings (standard LDS church
services), several people will typically "bear testimony,"
not infrequently with tears in their eyes, in language like,
"I know the Savior lives. . . . I know the Book of Mormon
is true. . . . I know Joseph Smith was a prophet of God. . . .
I know this is the one true Church."

Similarly, the semiannual General Conference meetings become occasions rife with inspirational feeling as
the LDS prophet and other top leaders speak, often with
very heartwarming stories, and the Mormon Tabernacle
Choir sings—all aimed to help the members maintain
their testimony by a deluge of confirmational feelings.
There are even many stories of ecstatic experiences in the
temple, sometimes in the midst of the rituals, sometimes
involving the appearance of dead relatives who "testify"
from beyond the grave that the LDS Church is true! I even
watched and heard with my own eyes and ears as a good
Mormon friend of ours talked to an LDS youth class and
closed with a riveting, tender story of a Mormon leader
who had "the Savior" physically appear to him while he
prayed in the temple one day! This concluding story left
the class in a sanctified hush full of deep feeling—quite
understandably, wouldn't you say?

Paralysis of Analysis or Divine Romance?

Of course, traditional Christians may intellectually dispute the validity of the LDS epistemology of romanticism, believing it to be inadequate or ill founded or even potentially deceitful. And many Christians proceed to bring this dispute into their evangelistic approach to Mormons, voicing such frontal statements as, "But you can't trust feelings as a basis for truth! Feelings are tricky. They lead gullible people into cults with strong leaders (like David Koresh or Jim Jones) and suicide pacts and all the rest!"

Let me make some observations. In almost every case, this argument, if voiced to most Mormons, will not only fail to make their trust in this epistemology go away, but worse, it will simply raise defenses and barriers to your conversation with them. Defenses will go up because they will feel this is one more "persecution" or attack on their faith in the long history of outsiders attacking them. And perhaps most importantly, no matter what anyone else thinks of it, their romantic epistemology will remain a deeply entrenched cultural fact. Whether we like it or not, this way of knowing has been profoundly trained into their modus operandi at deep, culturally ingrained, even subconscious levels, despite any argument brought against it on the cognitive level.

Often, then, our problem boils down to our tendency to speak of spiritual things analytically to ears trained in hearing romantically. Perhaps we explicate biblical doctrines well supported by chapter and verse, like the notion of God justifying us while we were still sinners by grace through faith in Christ alone, as Romans 5:8 and Ephesians 2:8–9 plainly show. Then we proceed to argue that this does not square with the LDS view of gaining exaltation, and we find our tightly woven case falls on deaf ears! We may often hear our Mormon friend reply, simply and respectfully, something like this: "That is a very good argument and I can respect your belief, but I could not embrace it because I have a testimony in my heart that what the LDS Church teaches is true and so I *know* it's true." The testimony, remember, is a matter of intense, experienced feelings. In knowing what is true in spiritual matters, feelings trump arguments. Direct experience triumphs over doctrinal explanation.

A quick, easy way to see abundant examples of the centrality of feelings in Mormon testimonial discourse is to consult the LDS Church website at www.lds.org, click on the "Church Publications" link, and do a search using the phrase "bear my testimony." Doing this will reward you with well over three hundred articles—mostly from LDS magazines—in which this pervasive language of experience and feeling occurs. Let's look at just a few excerpts from these stories:

> I found the *Book of Mormon* and began to read. When I finished reading, I prayed with all my heart. I felt a warmth in my heart and a burning in my chest.
>
> My life turned around. I began to pray, fast, bear my testimony, preach the gospel to my coworkers, pay tithing, and read and study the holy scriptures. I felt happy and close to my Heavenly Father.[2]

> Sister Wallace nodded. "You bore a beautiful testimony, Adam, and I could tell that you meant every word. But tell me, what special thing did you receive?"
>
> "It was a special feeling," I said. "I can't explain it, but it felt real good."
>
> "That's exactly what I knew you'd receive," said Sister Wallace. "That feeling was the Holy Ghost letting you know that what you were saying was true."[3]

> The next fast Sunday, I fasted to know if the *Book of Mormon* was true. . . . Testimony meeting was going along great that day. I was even happy for Molly Prentiss when she went up and bore her testimony. Then Brother Badger went to the front to speak. His quiet voice trembled as he spoke of his great love for the scriptures and how he knew the truth of the gospel.

As he spoke, a strange feeling started in a little spot in my chest. It got warmer and bigger until my whole body was filled with glowing, tingly warmth. When he finished, that warmth seemed to pick me up and carry me right to the pulpit. The lump in my throat loosened into a few words that came right from the soul: "I know that the *Book of Mormon* is true. In the name of Jesus Christ, amen."[4]

I remember a series of discussions I had with two Mormon college students a number of years ago. I proposed we study the book of Galatians, and I came prepared to deliver my airtight case that Paul's argument in the book for the gospel of grace as he understood it would rule out the Mormon "gospel," because he would dismiss it as "another gospel," a different gospel from the one the apostles preached. The students listened politely, then unblushingly replied that they felt I was the one proclaiming "another gospel," because no matter what I had to say, the LDS Church today has the restored gospel of the original apostles. Furthermore, they did not just "believe" this to be true but, as one of them put it with great emphatic force, "I *know* it is true because *I have a testimony* of it." I went away tremendously deflated and bewildered, taking solace in the typical proof text about Satan "blinding their eyes." Even if they were blinded, I was blindsided. I had no clue how to respond!

Ken Mulholland remembers a similar adventure—or misadventure, as the case may be—from his early days in Utah.

Thirty years ago, I had great confidence in the power of argument to persuade LDS people that their truth-claims were false. I believed that if I could just show them that they were wrong about their confidence in Joseph Smith, in their new revelations, or in their church, then they would quickly accept my beliefs in the authority of the Bible, in the Triune God, and in salvation by faith alone. I'm not sure why I assumed this, but I did. In my first few years in

Utah, I steadfastly pursued this approach. I was dedicated to knowing as many facts as I could so that I could tear down the foundations of the beliefs of LDS people.

Finally, I became convinced that I had the unassailable argument—the Silver Bullet—that would overthrow any "reasonable" Mormon's confidence in Mormon doctrine. I shared this argument with two returned LDS missionaries. They were polite and listened with great interest. After I had finished what I thought to be a compelling presentation, I asked them what they thought. They looked at me with great sincerity and said thoughtfully that my argument was solid and good. But, in the final analysis, they could not accept its conclusion because they had both prayed about the Mormon faith and they had a "testimony" that it was true.

I was stunned by their response. I could see that they really did understand my arguments and they saw that these arguments had intellectual power. They even seemed respectful that my presentation was not a wild attack on their faith, but reasoned and clear. However, they rejected my "knock down" argument with a quiet confidence that forever changed my life. Their response was that they knew the LDS Church was true because they felt it to be true. The text that is most often cited to support this appeal to feelings comes from the *Book of Mormon* (Moroni 10:3–5): "Ask God . . . if these things are not true . . . he will manifest the truth of it unto you, by the power of the Holy Ghost." Mormons are taught that God will confirm the truth of the LDS gospel by a "burning in the bosom." This warm feeling is the ultimate way of knowing truth for Latter-day Saints.[5]

The Evangelistic Obstacle Course

Like Ken and like myself, many traditional Christians have become aware (sometimes painfully) of barriers or obstacles to communicating the Good News with LDS people in a way that truly sounds like good news. There may also be a few unnamed barriers in this process—ones we have simply not thought about before. Let's consider some of these various kinds of obstacles.

1. *A very common barrier is ignorance or simple disbelief in the claim that this epistemology issue is a genuine problem.* A long and practiced legacy of traditional Christian church culture has cultivated an aversion to romantic orientation in dealing with gospel truth. This is *our* entrenched culture. We who received our training in this culture, especially we Western Protestants, tend to be oriented toward tightly rational, verbally textual statements as the normal way of conveying the truth about spiritual things. We are more at home with words and linear arguments than with images and experiences, more at home with propositional truth than with poetic truth. We'd rather argue from Romans or John than present the gospel as a dance or in a drama or in the form of our personal story. This is especially true for the part of "we" who are theologically educated in the West, and often it filters down from the church leaders so educated. We've been trained to deal more on the cognitive level than the affective level.

Now, the real problem here may not be our training so much as our assumption, usually unquestioned and un-examined, that this is indeed "the *normal* way of knowing and conveying truth" for everybody. Perhaps it doesn't even occur to us that our Mormon friends may not find this mode of operating normal at all! For my first several years of living in the Salt Lake City area, it certainly did not occur to me. As a result, I did what many of us do: I treated my LDS friends as two-dimensional information processors. I figured if I just blathered away at them with enough well-argued Bible verses, they would automatically get enlightened, fall to their knees, and repent. When nei-ther their minds nor their knees seemed to comply, I found myself roundly disillusioned, again and again. Now, don't misunderstand me here: I'm not talking about diminish-ing our confidence in the power of the Bible but about reframing our understanding of how that power actually works in some cases.

What I have needed and what many traditional Christians need is a serious awareness *with appreciation* of Mormon epistemology. This means more than overcoming our ignorance of the different way of knowing by which Mormon folk are taught to access spiritual truth. The term "appreciation" implies a willingness on our part to speak into their world, to start where they are rather than where we are, to walk a mile in their Nikes, to ferret out common denominators of experience and share the Good News in terms of that experience—in short, to "speak Mormonese." Briefly for now, let's say by way of example it may mean we begin to converse with our LDS friends much more (and more characteristically) by telling about a recent answer to prayer or a stunning act of God we've experienced or a gospel-like image from a film than by reciting a Bible verse or sharing a great doctrinal "insight" we got in last Sunday's sermon.

2. *A kind of cousin to the first barrier is fear of adapting to the LDS cultural epistemology at the imagined risk of compromising the gospel message.* While the above barrier doesn't see such adaptation as valid, this second barrier doesn't see it as healthy. There are those who even go further and see it as toxic. Many who resonate with this rationale have an uneasy anxiety about expressing feelings and experience as a mode for preaching the gospel, thinking the former will end up swallowing the latter. They may figure if experienced feelings become *something* in our methods, they will become *everything*. Besides, as some will argue, feelings of a "romantic glow" character can be tricky and mislead us into illusions of infatuation, but the gospel is the truth and should not be tainted by such a misleading way of knowing. Isn't the gospel a proclamation of God acting to save us in Christ, an accomplished fact regardless of how we feel? And if we start down this "language-of-experience" road, we just might obscure this

simple message and lead our LDS friends to worship their experience rather than the Jesus who saves us—to worship, as spiritual sages have put it, the consolations of God rather than the God of consolations!

While this kind of fear may indicate a very valid concern, even a demonstrable danger, I believe it most often is highly exaggerated or misplaced. And frankly, sometimes we harbor a deeper fear behind this fear of compromising the gospel. I'll make three observations.

In the first place, we are determining which facet of the gospel diamond we will present, not whether or not we will present the diamond. We are turning the gospel diamond to the facet that gleams with a certain brilliance, catching the very rays of heaven and sending them to a certain person or group because that facet appeals to a particular need they profoundly own. Jesus announced the gospel to the Samaritan woman (John 4) through the facet of his eternal wellspring of love that could satisfy the "thirst" for love in her life (five husbands and still not quenched!). He shared the gospel with the religious leader Nicodemus (John 3) through the facet of birth "from above" by the Spirit. Similarly, we will announce the same gospel through the facet that best appeals to those with whom we deal.

In the case of LDS people, the facet of romantic experience with the divine bridegroom proves tremendously compelling, so we learn to speak the language of our experienced love life with God to our Mormon friends. But at the same time, we recognize the limits of this way of announcing because we are aware it does not present the entirety of the gospel, only the gleaming facet that most appeals to our listeners (something true, by the way, of *every* facet). From this entry point, we can go on to tell the whole story when the time is appropriate.

Second, we should face the question of whether feelings and experience do indeed deceive people. They can. And some take flight from this danger into the pure, feelingless realm of correct intellectual doctrine, creedal formulation, "sound biblical teaching." Unfortunately, such folks fail to realize this path can deceive as well, so they place themselves in jeopardy of the equally dangerous (perhaps even more dangerous) trap of hard-hearted scribalism, that precise correctness with which the scribes held to the Word of God with legalistic rigor. Their "correctness" became such a fixation that their hearts could not be touched by the Good News of the kingdom of God when Jesus proclaimed it. Behind this tendency often lurks the ill-conceived assumption that our emotions are tainted by sin, but our minds are not. Yet the Bible clearly states that every part of our humanity participates in the fall—mind, emotions, will, body (check out the book of Romans, especially chapters 1, 3, and 7). We must simply learn to trust the Spirit of God who inspired the Scriptures to illumine them to our minds and ignite them in our hearts—and to do the same for our Mormon friends.

My third comment has to do with a deeper fear, which sometimes gets masked by the fear of feelings-orientation tainting our gospel proclamation. Some traditional Christians simply don't have much romance with God going on in their lives, and therefore they have little or nothing to say about their feelings and experience. And they may even, beneath it all, be rather afraid, perhaps even ashamed, to admit there's no real fire in their souls. Instead of rekindling that fire, it may seem a lot safer to stay on the level of memorized verses and intellectualized arguments. In short, it's easier to become a "Bible answer man" than a Bible-based man (or woman), easier to be correct than contrite, easier to master content than character, easier to be informed about Christ than formed by Christ. Sadly, folks who take this easier path end up coming across more like Scripture-spouting Stoics than like full-bodied, whole-souled Christians. My plea would be, for the sake of the incarnate Christ, let's relinquish enough of our fear of the emotional to simply and fully be human! I've always loved what Thomas à Kempis says in *The Imitation of Christ*: "I would rather feel contrition than know how to define it."[6] It will take people with just that attitude to minister the Good News to Mormon people in their own epistemological language.

3. *A third barrier rests on what I believe to be a misconstruing of the language-of-experience strategy, namely, that this is simply a "kinder, gentler" approach to evangelizing LDS people and it will not prove effective.* I've heard some even comment derogatorily that this approach is used by those who cave in to the pressures of "tolerance" and "political correctness" because they lack courage to stand for the truth. The barrier consists in a repudiation (or at least dismissal) of such a strategy in favor of what one gentleman called the "shock-and-awe" approach: LDS people, he believes, need (at least sometimes) to be confronted with the unsavory, deceitful, and even horrifying facts about their worldview and historical practices in the hopes this may move them to turn from Mormonism and repent. The "kinder, gentler" approach is in this view simply not strong enough medicine.

For example, one report from sound sources describes a hardened sheriff of LDS persuasion in southern Utah who visited the nearby excavation site of the terrible and shameful event in Mormon history known as the Mountain Meadows Massacre.[7] In 1857, on the ironic date of September 11, a wagon train of Arkansas farmers passing through this area en route to California to resettle was assaulted by a band of mostly Mormons who painted their bodies to look like Native Americans; the assailants killed in cold blood nearly 120 innocent people to avenge the blood of Joseph Smith, according to the best historical evidence.[8] As digging at the site progressed, bones of slaughtered men, women, and children were unearthed, and the sheriff was handed the skull of a two-year-old child with a bullet hole in it. Holding it, the horror of it all so engulfed him that he broke down and wept. This is "shock and awe" at work! Now, we must hasten to add that there is nothing in the account reporting that this man, understandably moved though he was, repented and left Mormonism to become a traditional Christian. But he was undeniably moved.

What compels us about this account and others like it is a stirring at the level of deep feelings: great emotions of revulsion and sorrow, no less than great emotions of tenderness and mercy, can move us deeply. Frankly, this method can be seen as a variation on the same theme we've been playing. Even though it moves toward a sort of "tough love" method, it can still register as an act of love and may therefore be perfectly appropriate under certain circumstances. No way do I, for one, believe all manifestations of God's grace are "gentle" or mushy sentimental: sometimes it comes in the form of Jesus rampaging through the temple or shouting "Woe to you, scribes and Pharisees, hypocrites!" But if we do this on occasion, let there be lament in our voices if not tears on our faces, for we must remember that Christians in the Crusades, Ireland, and Rwanda have had blood on their hands as well. There ought to be no quarter for self-righteous pontificating here. Righteous indignation we may experience, but that's very different from *self*-righteous indignation. Let's be people who come alongside that sheriff and weep *with* him, pleading for God's mercy on all of us!

Often what results from those who think this book's approach reflects a failure of nerve or lack of holy boldness is the following. In reacting to the straw figure they imagine as a kind of marshmallow evangelist operating under the cliché "kinder, gentler," these people make a professional duty (or holy mission) out of methods that are harsher, "holier" in "preaching the truth." They correct error in confrontational discourse or even in the loud, bombastic tones of headline-grabbing street preachers on the plaza in front of the Salt Lake Temple. Far more often than not, as I have observed these wannabe zealots for the Lord, the end result is a lot of self-congratulatory bombast bereft of wisdom, grace, forgiveness, and brokenheartedness. They may speak the truth, but they certainly fail to do so "in love" (see Eph. 4:15). Such approaches do not sound even remotely like good news! I often wonder if much of what parades as "boldness" is not actually just a bunch of unharnessed anger hurling imagined God-bombs at people with a sense of smug pride.

Truthfully, as I mentioned above, the term "kinder, gentler" would be a misnomer for what I advocate in this book. Much better might be a term like "wiser, gentler," taken from Jesus' advice to the twelve disciples he sent out on an evangelistic mission: "Be ye therefore wise as serpents, and harmless as doves" (KJV), or, in the NIV, "as shrewd as snakes and as innocent as doves" (Matt. 10:16). Coupled with this counsel is Paul's example of becoming "all things to all men so that by all possible means I might save some" (1 Cor. 9:22). The better part of the wisdom Jesus called for would engender evangelistic approaches filled with cultural awareness and shrewdness yet gentle. If we notice how he related to the Samaritan woman (John 4), we will see how he himself embodied this approach: wisely and gently he entered her world simply asking for a drink of water so he could talk about her "thirst" for the gospel, and yet his wise gentleness in no way interfered with his boldly proclaiming the truth to her about her need and God's answer to it.

In short, for those nervous about a failure of nerve in our evangelism, the lesson is plain: out of love, be bold and truthful in ways and times appropriate to what is *usually and normally* a wise and gentle proclamation of the Good News, just as our Lord himself modeled.

For our Mormon friends, this will truly make the Good News *sound like good news!* Strategically adapting to their culture, especially their romantic epistemology, we will "speak the truth in love" to our LDS friends so we may through the grace of God "by all possible means . . . save some."

For Discussion and More

1. "What does your heart tell you? Is your soul at peace?" Discuss thoughtfully and personally how questions like these (from the opening dialogue) *are* used when people talk about spiritual matters, and how they *can be* used by traditional Christians talking with Mormons. Are heart-language questions easy or hard for you to use and to answer? Why? What are the pros and cons?

2. Do you have experience-level knowledge of "nagging not-good-enoughness" or, as Redford puts it, "falling short . . . not making it . . . not able to do these things" when it comes to God's commandments? Talk about it. Tell how you can specifically resonate with people caught in this legalistic dilemma.

3. Tell about any experiences you may have had or heard about with "romantic epistemology"—experienced feelings as an indication that something in the spiritual realm is true. Are there ways traditional Christians use this way of knowing, and if so, how is it like and unlike the ways Mormons use it?

4. Discuss objections to using the language of experience with Mormon people when doing evangelism. If there are also other objections not mentioned in the chapter, bring them up and evaluate each claim. What drives the claim, and what pros and cons do you see as you evaluate it?

5. Study again the biblical statements mentioned earlier, and others like them, that apparently tell us God wants us to "wisely, gently" accommodate the form (not the content) of the gospel message to the cultural form of our hearers. Biblically, why would God want us to learn to "speak Mormonese"?

9

Speaking Mormonese

Stories and Sensibilities

Jane Christensen, clueless about any impropriety, stepped to the podium from her seat at the banquet. "I'd like to bear *my* testimony about how God has used this school in my life. I am a born again Mormon."

With little gulps of apprehension, we who were (sort of) in charge of the banquet just sat there a bit stunned and let her rip. The program we'd planned for the Biblical Institute's annual fund-raising-and-celebration event was coming off wonderfully. Some faculty and administrators had made their statements, music had been performed, and now the student speakers we'd recruited had finished their talks. But it seemed God had recruited one more than we had! So, utterly unsolicited, up stepped Jane.

To our delight—and not a few sighs of relief—she unraveled her personal story about being a practicing, committed Mormon who came to study the Bible at this evangelical school in Salt Lake City—a story that paid high tribute to "Heavenly Father" for using the school to deepen her and help her know him better. She was even at pains to emphasize she'd experienced "total acceptance" and "no criticism or Mormon bashing" at the institute. What Jane did *not* unravel was her meaning for the term "born-again Mormon." We're still wondering.

But we wonder in both senses—a curious pondering over whether she is "born again" in the way traditional Christians understand that term, and a curious marveling over God's way of doing more than we plan on (not just in the banquet but also in a student's life). Several of us at the seminary believe there's a strong likelihood she is indeed born again as traditional Christians define the term. But for our purposes, there's more to be mined from this experience. We observed a simple truth about our relationship with Jane: she had become comfortable enough with us to "bear testimony" because she had heard us speaking the Good News about God in her language. While several of us were scratching our heads over what had happened, one of us said, "Hey, it's testimony time!" We then and there remembered it's a universal practice of Mormon culture to offer a voluntary word of testimony during a meeting when others are testifying, so she felt perfectly comfortable jumping right in line! Others spoke the language of their experience, so she spoke hers. Furthermore, in her biblical studies, Jane had encountered the God of the Bible in fresh ways, and *that's* the kind of experience she was talking about.

The Shape of "Mormonese": Sense and Sensibility

What observations might we make about the language of experience Jane had been schooled by her culture to hear and speak? What does it look like? What is the shape of "Mormonese"? Let me offer some points of sensibility for this kind of language, that is, some particulars marking the form this strategy of discourse and action might take.

1. *Speak the Personal*

Let's intend our words to become, as much as possible, person-to-person rather than "Christian-to-Mormon." For example, I always ask permission to know the first names of Mormon missionaries who visit our door, as I mentioned earlier, and then deal with them on a first-name basis—something very few people at the homes they visit will do. Ultimately, despite differences of culture, Mormons are people just like us. Let's reach into their lives at a level below the name tags, below the roles of members of different churches or persons with different beliefs, to where our common humanity exists. Let's let our words reach into the place of beating hearts, where their loves and fears reside, their aspirations and exasperations, their dreams and pains and dancing joys. Of course, to do this fully and faithfully we will need to be open, even vulnerable, about these heartfelt elements of our own lives as well.

For a brief time, our local Albertsons grocery store experimented with a coffee-and-ice-cream counter. It was friendly, sociable, and had a certain hometown charm in which you could loosen up and converse with other customers or the person behind the counter. We loved it, but within less than a year the management pulled it out because coffee doesn't "market" well in our 93 percent Mormon town. In the meantime, Hazel and I struck up a relationship with Marie, a nice thirtysomething Mormon lady who usually worked at the counter to fix our lattes and cappuccinos. Soon we began talking with her about our lives—our kids, our church life, Hazel's penchant for theater, my excitement over nearing the end of Ph.D. work, our marriage being stressed to the breaking point, God rescuing us, and so on. She shared likewise with us.

One day Marie responded to the typical "How's it going?" opener with a "Not so well." We asked if she cared to share with us and, since we were the only ones at the counter and she'd come to trust us on this very personal level, she opened up. She told us her marriage was ending due to her husband's drug habit that made her fear for her children. After listening with concern for a while and discussing her options, I leaned over the counter, engaged her eyes fully, and in a near whisper said, "Marie, we share your heaviness in this. We know it's hard, and how much this hurts you. Hazel and I will be praying for you because we also know our Lord cares for you even more than we do. Here's my card. Call if you need help or just to talk. Or we'll see you here again and be interested in how things develop—and how our prayers for you get answered." Marie began to cry as we got ready to leave. Over the next few months, we saw her through the breakup and prayed a lot, and I believe an indelible mark was left on her soul for the sake of the gospel.

2. Hear the Hunger

If we want our words to count by making a real impact for the gospel so those Mormons who do not know Christ can come to know him, as a rule we should start not with Joseph Smith or polygamy or false prophecies or unbiblical doctrine but with whatever spiritual hunger is in their lives. (A small caveat: sure, respond to doctrinal questions if asked, but humbly, artfully, nonconfrontationally. Sometimes, though rarely, these *are* how your friend shows a spiritual hunger.) Listen carefully to your Mormon friend: beneath the noises about prophets, "the Savior," and church activities, you will eventually hear the growling of hunger pangs. As Pastor Ross Anderson, a former Mormon, puts it:

> You know, I think in our evangelism we put the cart before the horse when we emphasize theological truth first, or try to identify a particular theological key that's going to open the door to bridge our witness to Mormons. I think we have to start with the spiritual hunger, the spiritual thirst, because I'm assuming that Mormons like any human beings

are created in the image of God, that they have eternity in their hearts, and so therefore they have the capacity and some inherent desire to know God. . . . Mormons have the capacity to be spiritually thirsty, but until they really are, theological discussions, while they may help them understand me better and me understand them better, are really not that fruitful in terms of leading someone to Christ.[1]

This is precisely what Jesus did when he evangelized the Samaritan woman. Rather than discussing the questionable orthodoxy of her people worshipping on a certain mountain or in a certain way, he started with a discussion of "thirst" by talking about a kind of thirst he can permanently satisfy and then saying, "Go, call your husband," which brought to the surface her spiritual thirst (or hunger pangs) for love.

My very good friend James grew up in a Mormon family and experienced the same hunger pangs as the Samaritan woman all through his childhood and young adulthood. He once told me, "It was not until I was nineteen years old, sitting one Sunday in a Baptist church in Southern California, that I really heard for the first time in my life that God loves me." James was talking about *unconditional* love, which had been a foreign concept in his culture of conditional grace (God loves you *if* . . . you follow the commandments, pay your tithe, go to church, and so on). It was a foreign concept indeed, but also the hunger of his heart.

Whatever the spiritual hunger in our friend's life—for love, for joy, for truth, for worthiness—let's listen for it, identify it, and start there.

3. Show Real Respect

One of the passions of my heart as I've lived here these years in Utah and ministered is to live here with a sense of respect, even though there may be some deep disagreements and deep convictions on both sides. But if we can live in mutual respect, then that will be good for all of us together, and also will open the door for us to really talk and interact with each other and share our faith on a level that is not demeaning but on a level that will encourage people to examine the claims of Christ, examine the claims of the Bible.[2]

That was spoken by Les Magee of Washington Heights Baptist Church in Ogden, Utah. The church he pastored before he retired has practiced this attitude consistently and had phenomenal growth, 25 to 30 percent of the new members being former Mormons. If the language our Mormon friends and neighbors hear from us is void of bashing, slighting, belittling, and ridicule and full of honor, curious interest, and appreciation, it will open doors into their lives for the gospel.

Two corollaries pertain here. As Magee continues, "Be a genuine friend to them. Let them know that you really care about them and that you're not just interested in converting them to your faith, but you care about them as a person." Don't relate to them, in other words, as merely an "evangelistic prospect" but as a true friend, regardless of the spiritual commitments they make. Furthermore, we should honestly and humbly realize we have things to learn from them! Their industry, organizing effectiveness, helpfulness to neighbors, missionary zeal, and other qualities are quite commendable.

4. Seize Common Ground

The language of experience most familiar and common to LDS people will be the language of story and song, drama and symbol, myth and parable. As Jesus spoke in parables, so should we, and with our Mormon friends, this becomes common ground. Give your own story of meeting, knowing, and walking with Jesus. Take your friends to a Christian concert. Lend them a CD. Talk through a parable, like the one about the Pharisee and the tax collector, or the one about the workers in the vineyard hired at various times of the day but all paid exactly the same, or the story of the prodigal sons[3] (some of my favorites to use). Theater provides a wonderful venue for our friends. Dinner theaters in churches have successfully drawn in large numbers of LDS people and in the nonthreatening language of drama presented the Good News of the Bible to them. And here's another way to seize common ground using theater. Several years ago my family members and I acted in a local community theater production of the musical *Fiddler on the Roof*. We made several relationships with people in the cast. Near the end of the run, I got permission for our church to host the cast members and their families for a "Fiddler Sunday." We strategically chose a weekend of the semiannual LDS Conference, when the Mormons do not schedule their regular church meetings. We invited the cast, and they turned out in droves—I mean, it was standing room only! I preached out of the book of Hebrews about the Jewish heritage of Christian faith, and we gave testimonies of appreciation for the cast and held a matzo-ball soup lunch for everyone. There was much feasting and merriment, appreciation for our friends, a praise-song time they adored, and witness to the biblical story of redemption. They are still talking about it today!

5. Let It Shine

In front of our Mormon friends, let's be natural about our spiritual experience and spiritual about our natural experience. What I mean here is, let your life in Christ shine so your LDS friends hear the language of *your* experience. For example, pray overtly as well as covertly for your LDS friends, tell the story of how you met Christ, testify to God's actions and messages to you in your everyday life, speak of news events with a providential frame because God's in control of his world, and tell of his comfort and righteousness in the midst of tragedy.

I know friends who pray for people at the drop of a hat, and yes, I mean out loud in front of them if the occasion permits, perhaps with a hand on their shoulder. They find Mormon people especially love this in-the-moment experiential ministry of the Lord's presence. I've been led by the Lord to do the same thing on many occasions, and I find the same response.

Once an elderly and quite sickly man came to our house to make a delivery for his business. This nice LDS man was coughing and sputtering and limping, and as I was paying the bill, I asked if I could pray for him. He answered that he goes to the temple sometimes, and some people offer prayers for his chronic condition. "Okay," I said, "but I mean right now, right here, may I pray for you? I know the Lord's concerned for your body as well as your soul. Would you feel okay about that?"

"Why, yes, that would be fine." I bowed my head and offered a normal, conversational prayer for him in the natural way I talk with God. After the amen, he looked up at me and said with a tone of astonishment, "That was a *wonderful* prayer. Thank you."

I said, "It was simply a *real* prayer. I wasn't trying to be wonderful—God just wants to hear our hearts. We'll look for his answer."

That kind of astonishment and wonder at the powerful, intimate relationship we have with our Lord is often shown by Mormons, as everyone I know who does this kind of direct ministry will tell you. This is the language of experience in action—"speaking Mormonese" at its best!

"Mormonese" in Action: Some God-Ordained Experiences

"You know, I felt like *God* was there!" That was the response when my colleague Ken Mulholland asked what his Mormon friend thought of the worship service they'd just attended at Ken's church. At his invitation, she'd gone to a traditional Christian church for the first time in her life. Her voice sounded full of surprise, as if she didn't think this was supposed to happen in a non-LDS church. Ken responded to her comment quite simply: "You know why? Because he *was*." Notice what happened after that, as Ken tells it, and the sense he makes of it:

> And that was a turning point in her life. *She* came to the point of saying, "I have theological questions I'd like to ask you. What about Joseph Smith? What about the Book of Mormon?" At that point, she was really wanting to be disentangled from the doctrinal issues that she had. But we had to go through the experience of her *feeling* that Christianity was valid and true, and at that point the intellectual questions and the theological questions rose to the forefront.[4]

Carol Jensen recalls the time she went at the invitation of her boss to a Christian concert by The Continentals. She says it struck her as kind of "odd" because as the group performed, people all around her were "praising God and, I mean, they've got their hands over their head." Then she describes, in what has to be one of the two or three most beautifully transparent, compelling accounts I've ever heard by a transitioning Mormon, her experience of tension between bewilderment (even dismissive distaste) and attraction—a classic kind of epiphany:

> And this little guy that was just as irritating as everything, sitting in front of us, just, as he went into that song he just closed his eyes, his hands were in the air, he was swaying—it was just—very disorienting. But then, his pure love for Jesus—everyone around us kind of got into this, and their love—and I could see this love for Jesus, and I really, my heart was breaking, because I thought, "they're in the kindergarten of religion—I'm in the university getting my upper degrees, and just for a minute I'd like to just put it

aside and be free to just sing about Jesus and love him like that." Seeing this love, it's just very different for Mormons; and it also related back to when I was a child and had sung those songs. One of the things that Christians can show to Mormons [is] that as they expose their love for Jesus, it's just so *surprising* to Mormons—how can they fail to just want to be free to do that?[5]

Finally, let me share about a Mormon to whom, in this case, God himself spoke in "Mormonese." The story of my friend Jan Castro's conversion figures as the most dramatic I've ever witnessed close up. In this case, I had a front-row seat at a God show I'll never forget.

Dave Castro and his wife, Jan, came the first night to a class I was to teach at the seminary—a class titled "How We Got the Bible." Only three students showed up, and our normal policy is to cancel a class if there are less than five, although it's a professor's call. I gave the first lecture, promptly announced the class would be canceled, and dismissed them after prayer.

The Castros stayed to talk, however, and I took the opportunity to ask about the two of them, including questions about their spiritual journey. They said they'd been married only a few years, both were medical professionals, and . . . "How long have you been a Christian, Dave?" I asked.

"Since I was eight. I was converted at a Bible camp and raised spiritually in the Nazarene Church, but then I fell away for many years. For the past six years or so I've been trying to follow God seriously again."

"And, Jan, how long have *you* been a Christian?"

"Well, um . . . I'm not one," she said sheepishly. "I'm a lifelong Mormon, and, well, Dave and I are both seeking for what God wants in our church life and for what his truth is about. We've agreed to pray for wisdom and to visit each other's churches—both traditional Christian and LDS—but not discuss the issues for now because it gets argumentative. I was *so looking forward* to this class because I really want to know if I can fully trust the Bible like Christians do, despite its translation errors and all. Is there any way it could continue?"

Something happened inside me at this moment, which I'm now convinced was a Holy Spirit nudging. I now understood why their faces had fallen with visible disappointment when I announced the cancellation of the class. "Well . . . maybe. Tell you what. Let me pray about this for a couple days and call you before next week's scheduled class session. Perhaps the Lord wants us to go ahead with this class." Perhaps also, I didn't tell them, I was using a favorite Christian hedging device to buy time for . . . something, but *what?* It seemed like I already had my answer: God was clearly on the move in these two lives, and the class was to be an important part of what he was doing. In short, I was already beginning to feel negligent toward him by canceling it. Still, confirmation through prayer can't hurt, I reasoned (or rationalized).

That was Monday night. By Wednesday, after many prayers had gone up from my heart and those of several friends I enlisted, I still had that little Jonah cloud of discomfort and negligence haunting me whenever I thought of canceling the class. "Okay, Lord," I finally said, "I'm your servant. We'll do it." That evening I called Dave and Jan and the third student to tell them the class was on.

Now we get to see the other half of God's agenda, the part we didn't plan on, which opened up because we said yes to the first part. The Saturday of the third week of class, we held a daylong prayer retreat at the seminary, open to anyone for a small fee but free to students taking classes that term. I was leading the retreat. Both Dave and Jan came.

For an opener, I like to use a simple prayer exercise we do as a group even though it leads each one into very personal prayer in silence. I got it from Richard Foster's *Celebration of Discipline*; it's called "Palms Down, Palms Up."[6] It works like this. As prayer leader, I first ask the group members to sit upright with their eyes closed and hands resting on their laps, palms down. Then I guide them into a piece of imagery: "Picture yourself holding the handle on a piece of luggage with your hands. Raising them up a couple inches, physically clench them around that handle. In the brief time of silence that follows, recognize that luggage as a weight in your life that you've been carrying, like an unconfessed sin, a worry, perhaps a broken relationship you mourn, whatever. Ask the Lord to show you what he wants to. As we are silent now, picture a label on the side of that luggage that names your particular weight, your burden. Then in faith simply release your grasp, and see yourself dropping it into God's lap, remembering he tells us in his Word to cast all your cares on him, for he cares for you." After a generous moment's silence, I then tell them to continue in prayer, eyes still closed, by turning their hands over, palms upward and open in a receiving posture. I then guide them to picture themselves, in another time of silence, asking for and receiving a gift from their Lord to replace the burden they just released—for example, a gift of peace to replace their worry, a gift of reconciliation for a broken relationship—because Jesus told us in the Sermon on the Mount to ask our Father for his good gifts, knowing he loves to give them even much more than earthly fathers do. I tell them to use the silence to see themselves receiving the gift and thanking God for it. Finally, after more silence, I conclude with a prayer of gratitude, and we sing a song.

After this opener, my practice is to dismiss the group members for a two-hour time of solitude, during which they are to observe a rule of silence, are free to wander about the grounds or sit in a room, and are to seek the Lord in prayer. I give them resources to use if needed. I also offer to listen and intercede for any individuals who wish to visit me in the glassed-in front office.

You guessed it: in came Jan Castro, only minutes after the solitude began. She's a shy person and had to kick herself to do this, but right away she said she'd had a powerful encounter with God and thought I ought to know about it. Now at this point let me interject something: usually people who come in to talk about that opening exercise name some small- to middle-weight issue like concern over a cross word they uttered at their mother-in-law or worry about a job interview. With Jan, I was about to have my soul rocked, and I mean something in the range of 6.0 on the spiritual Richter scale.

She began by offering her initial misgivings about the experience because "the vision that came to me didn't exactly fit the images you described." That's when I got my first clue: if my suspicions were right, God himself had taken hold and was doing something much bigger than either of us anticipated. I reassured her it was fine if the vision didn't fit and asked her to continue.

"When you told us to picture a piece of luggage, what came to me was not like an overnight bag or suitcase with a handle but a very clear picture of a huge, brown burlap sack. It was filled with slips of paper that had rules and laws on them and also listed my 'works.' And instead of holding it by a handle, I was under it, holding it up with my hands and arms outstretched, and stumbling beneath its weight." Now she *really* had my attention, but this was nothing compared to what followed. "You told us to ask God to show us what it represented and see a label on the side, so I did. I looked up, and in large, black, bold letters on the side of the bag, I read the word 'MORMONISM.' Actually, I tried to change my thought into something like a sin that you were talking about, but the image wouldn't go away, so I decided to stick with it. It represented, I knew, a burden I'd carried—not just for some short time lately, but for my entire life. In fact, everything in my life was tied up in it—religious commitments, activities, values, family, raising children, *everything*!

"Anyway, you told us next to just let go of it and give it to God. I tried, but I couldn't do it! In my vision I found myself trying to push it away, but it wouldn't release. My hands were stuck to it as if they were superglued! Next I tried lowering it to the ground and kicking it with everything I had, but all this was still useless. I actually made up a mountain in my imagination after that, and I tried to kick it down the hill—but it just wouldn't go anywhere! I really wanted to let go, but it was like letting go of my whole life. I was stuck." Here she chuckled a bit at the slightly embarrassing oddness of this image, and I permitted myself to chuckle with her just a little.

"Then it came to me," she continued. "Just like all my life I'd been trained to 'take responsibility' and do things in my own strength, I was even trying to do this 'letting go' in my own strength—but its hold on me was so strong I couldn't overpower it!"

By now I was flabbergasted. What to do? I wasn't even sure how to counsel her.

Fortunately, God took care of that too, for Jan continued: "It came to me like a small voice that I should just ask God to take it away by *his* strength, *his* power. So I did, saying, 'Okay, Lord, you take it,' and the instant I prayed that, the entire sack floated away into the sky like a feather caught in a strong updraft! I mean, it just rose up into the clouds and disappeared like it was nothing!"

My jaw dropped.

"Then you told us to receive some gift from God to replace the burden we had just released," she continued. "The only thing that came to me in that moment was, this was the time I was to invite Jesus Christ to *personally* come in and take over my life—something I had never done but was the only thing God wanted me to do, right then. So I did. I asked God to fill my emptiness and *felt Jesus enter my heart*. The feeling was so powerful that I knew it was real. I had no doubt that it was his love. It felt like he put his arms around me and held me like a little child on his lap, and I knew that he had come into my life and that I had been 'born again' to a new life in Jesus Christ."

What filled *me* at this point was an awe that almost made me fall prostrate, right down on my face. Far beyond anything I could orchestrate, God had moved in with his mighty grace and spoken to Jan Castro in her native "Mormonese," the language of experience—visionary symbols, images, feelings, and all—so he could give her the gift of salvation in Christ.

At the end of the day, we regathered in our large group to share what we'd seen and heard God do. I had urged Jan to push herself a bit, overcome her shyness, and share this story with the group. When she did, I watched with profound joy as her husband, sitting next to her, began to cry. Thus began their new life in Christ together. Through the years I've followed them as they joined a Christ-centered, Bible-based church, became leaders, and went on mission trips yearly to serve Jesus with their medical skills and more among poor people in Central America.

I *still* marvel. At our precious Lord's workings, my soul fixates with wonder. I weep as I write.

For Discussion and More

1. Talk about personal-level concerns you have, "spiritual" or not, that become common ground with any Mormon friends or relatives you know. If you don't know any LDS people, what in your life *could become* such common ground with a Mormon? Can you list at least two or three items (practices, experiences, ethics, hopes, dreams, concerns)?
2. From your personal experience or what you've heard from others, what are some of the spiritual hungers or thirsts LDS people manifest?
3. Pick a parable of Jesus, and practice retelling it. Include nuances you're aware of, character insights, and personal connections you have to the story. For example, in the prodigal sons' story (Luke 15), when

the "unworthy" son has the "ring" put on his finger, that's a special ring used to seal business documents, so it's like the father just handed him the family checkbook! When you tell the story, emphasize how God has impacted *you* through it.

4. Discuss why (as in the example of Ken's friend) *"feeling* Christianity is true" would normally need to come first, before learning correct theology, in a Mormon's turning to Christ.

5. For either the Carol Jensen anecdote or the Jan Castro conversion story, discuss *what* elements constituted "speaking Mormonese" and *why* they led to such a profound moment of change in that person's life.

10

Concluding the Journey

Is Your Church a Safe Harbor?

Sometimes dramatically, sometimes not, we see an increasing number of Mormons making the transition to . . . well, to *what?* And particularly for the Christ-seeking journeyers who come from a life entrenched in Mormon culture, what does the road look like? How can we help them transition successfully into their new life? This last piece is where we must start as we draw our study to a conclusion: we must figure out how to help these pilgrims toward their (earthly) destination point, namely, incorporation into a local body of Christ—a grace-based community of fellow travelers.

Roadblocks and Remedies

Put yourself in the shoes of a Jan Castro, a Paul Murphy, or a Carol Jensen for a few minutes, and try to imagine what this journey really is like. Numerous roadblocks big and small must be overcome. They occur both on the

147

section of road leaving Mormonland and on the section entering traditional Christianland. They look something like this (some of them, at least).

Security and familiarity will be lost. The LDS structure automatically answered many questions and had clearly defined cultural roles and expectations. Besides, the tight-knit world of ward and family network provided a secure place for you to find your niche. Much of your life has been organized around Church activities. *Now* what?

Anger and bitterness may set in. Sometimes former Mormons feel they've been misled, even deceived—and to boot, it's at the hands of "the one true Church"! My friend Judi simply said, "For a long time I was eaten up with bitterness." You would not be alone if you felt like Judi, or like Wayne Jensen did at first: "We will *never* be suckered again."[1]

Threats and negative reactions from LDS friends, family members, and church officials may dog your steps. This often begins to happen even when you simply express doubts in any public way. The bishop may call you in to find out what moral or spiritual failure is causing you to "lose your testimony." From him or others you may receive threats that if you keep up your questioning, you'll split up the eternal family, and the Holy Ghost will leave you. You may lose friendships; if your spouse remains faithful as a Mormon and you do not, you may lose your marriage (not an uncommon occurrence).

Where do you fit in traditional Christianland, anyway? All the colors and flavors and styles of Christian churches—so far from the apparent uniformity of the Mormon Church—seem confusing. Do you go formal like Catholics, Episcopalians, and Lutherans, or informal like Baptists, Bible churches, and Pentecostals? And besides, just why do they do things the way they do—everything from taking the offering to serving wine or grape juice in the communion ceremony to getting "slain in the Spirit" and falling to the floor?

Just what do you believe, and where did you get it from? Your head may for a year or two be a jumble of doctrinal ideas, some Mormon, some biblical—and you can't tell which is which.

A profound loneliness can settle on you. Not only has your new faith in Christ perhaps alienated you from LDS family and friends; to exacerbate your loneliness, people in a biblical church you attend may be slow to connect with you and can't understand you very well. Besides, where are those home teachers to at least visit you and stay in touch? In Christianland, it can feel like you're on your own.

So, if you've walked a mile in their shoes, what does it feel like? What kinds of responses and initiatives by your new friends in God's "community of grace" would you hope to see?

Now let's put our own shoes back on—the footwear of traditional Christianity—and figure out what responses we can make to smooth the road for our new siblings in the faith from Mormonland. Okay, here are some remedies for those roadblocks.

Bring LDS friends to your church as soon and often as you can, to integrate them as fully as possible. These friends may be serious transitioners looking for a traditional Christian church, or less serious, or even LDS friends who have not yet "crossed the line" to faith in Christ but are open and curious enough to visit your church. Host them, keep them at your elbow, "big brother" (or "big sister") them, introduce them around, and help them make connections. Especially connect them with any other former Mormons in your congregation, because they've probably traveled the same road and can help greatly. Be in touch frequently. Find or initiate ministries and relational pockets that are "safe zones" for transitioning LDS folk—safe for asking odd questions and looking clueless and working through anger issues among people with whom they feel a real sense of belonging. The big objective is to see them fully, joyfully involved and identified with this new family in Christ. When it truly becomes *their* family, struggles with anger and feelings of loneliness will be remedied.

Help them past their anger so broken hearts replace bitter ones. Serious, vibrant, soulful worship is invaluable here, worship that humbles us before the mighty hand of God and opens us to taste his mercy and forgiveness again and again and again. This reshapes us to form in us his own merciful heart toward even those we feel have deceived us. Also, as mentioned above, fellow travelers help a lot. This can be a slow process, so be patient and sensitive toward your LDS friends in the congregation who are fighting this battle.

Accept, accept, accept! This is the manifesto of grace, the heart of the gospel of Christ, and the ultimate antidote to all who suffer rejection by friends, family, and authority figures. It must take on flesh, though! It will, if we have integrity about the gospel of grace we preach, which incarnates itself as new friends to embrace, pastoral care to heal, "safe zones" to open up in, helping hands for physical needs, prayer circles to bear the traveler up, and more.

Be prepared for lots of questions and little commitment from transitioning Mormons. At least at first, they may be reticent to fully plunge in—and for good or at least very understandable reasons. Some may wonder if your church's style and doctrinal stance are really best for them; some may move slowly because of a thin-ice relationship with a devout LDS spouse or other family member(s); some may have lingering notions from LDS culture, more subconscious than conscious, about what a "true church" needs to look like (Where are the "prophets and apostles"? Why are ministers paid?); some may simply watch and wait to see if the congregation is authentic and has "real" people and a basic integrity about its biblical faith practices—especially if they feel they've been burned. Do not be surprised if these journeyers sit in the back pew and observe for a long time, ask a lot of questions about why you "do church" they way you do, or even just camp with your church a short season and then move on in their "church shopping." Be patient with them and obedient to the Lord in helping them find their niche, even if it's elsewhere. Remember to give a lot of freedom and space for diverse options in the kingdom of God.

Offer and encourage involvement in teaching ministries, especially ones that provide basic biblical grounding. Some of these may be short courses or even weekend seminars, but some of them *must* be ongoing Bible study formats that cover in depth the foundational themes and truths of the Bible. Examples of the former are short courses like the Alpha series, a pastor's class for inquirers and new members on "what our church believes," a Walk Thru the Bible seminar, or a Via de Cristo (or Emmaus Walk) retreat. Examples of the latter are longer classes that go through basic Bible doctrines or books of the Bible like Genesis, John, Romans, or Galatians. Simply teaching former Mormons how to study the Bible inductively, listening and looking carefully for what it really says in its own context, is invaluable to helping them become biblical people. Broader Christian networks like Bible Study Fellowship can also be excellent for this inductive training and the learning of biblical literature. Some churches in areas of predominantly Mormon population offer courses comparing and contrasting Bible teaching to Mormon teaching. When done with great care to fully and accurately describe both worldviews with *no hint* of "Mormon bashing," this is a wonderful help toward grounding Mormons in transition.

This kind of ministry over a period of at least two or three years should clear away most of the fog former Mormons often have over where their understanding of certain doctrines (baptism for the dead? priesthood? exaltation? grace and works?) really comes from. In whatever format, basic biblical understanding of these four major issues is especially crucial: who God is, the person and mission of Jesus Christ, the nature of humankind, and the way of salvation.

We need to consider what it means to be a new family to those who come into our churches from a background in Mormon culture. Most often they've had to uproot from their former religious family, a process not atypically involving roadblocks with pain, confusion, loneliness, and a sense of being adrift. Let's learn to welcome them in and be a new home for them, a household of grace.

For churches located in areas where extensive and frequent ministry to Mormons is an opportunity, it's worth getting the leadership together to put into writing—after prayerful consideration of what God is leading you to do—an intentional philosophy of ministry your church will pursue regarding Mormons in transition. For example, some churches I'm aware of have a policy about pulpit rhetoric that includes a ban on any mention of other churches by name, especially "Mormon" as a general rule, to avoid creating any perception of "Mormon bashing"; some hold, as an intentional, ongoing ministry practice, regular classes on the Bible and Mormon doctrine; some offer at regular intervals the video training seminar I've cited a lot in this book—Bridges: Helping Mormons Discover God's Grace—to sensitize and inform the Christians in their congregation (or a cluster of congregations) about ministry to LDS people; and some have an intentional plan for assimilation of new people, with a special part of that plan addressing the needs of transitioning Mormons, like the need to be introduced to other former Mormons, to get involved in a Bible class, and so on.

These kinds of ministries and initiatives, offered by a local community of God's grace in Christ, will help our transitioning LDS friends immensely in overcoming the roadblocks on their journey. Most important in all of the above is the need for significant relationships to be formed, serious worship to be experienced, and sustained Bible teaching to be inculcated.

In Summary: On Learning a More Excellent Way

So, our journeyers may have successfully arrived in their new "home" by the grace of God through his people. As a final exercise, let's remind ourselves how these journeyers got there. Let's step back and look at the big picture. Let's focus on the broad brushstrokes of lessons in learning "a more excellent way" than traditional Christians have historically used for bringing the Good News of God's grace to Mormons.

In the final analysis, what can we make of the statements, stories, and scenarios we've considered in this book? To return to the opening vignettes, a study in contrast, what did Coach Scott McKinney do right that I and many others seemed to miss? Speaking for myself, as I look back at my track record, I'm truly sorry for the many confrontational, insensitive, sometimes bashing moves I've made toward LDS people. And I know many other traditional Christians can resonate with, even own, these apologetic and regretful feelings. Now, of course it's not as black-and-white as I told it, and you've probably guessed right if you figure I've overdrawn those anecdotes a bit to teach by hyperbole. Even when I didn't know it, there were times in relationships with neighbors when, I can see in retrospect, I "did it right" by God's grace; indeed, I recall the time our back-fence neighbors—*very* active Mormons—stunned Hazel and me by stating, "You're the most Christlike people we know." I believe most evangelicals who move here "do it right" at times, just as I believe Scott himself would tell you he *didn't* always "do it right." But in terms of intentional, committed, ongoing patterns of behavior vis-à-vis Mormon people—what I'd like to call our *prevailing praxis* (set of habitual practices)—what can we learn?

For one thing, *Mormons are people too!* By this I mean they are three-dimensional people, not two-dimensional information processors. Scott acted like the former is true; I had acted like the latter is true. And frankly, the history of the prevailing praxis of most traditional Christians in their encounters with Mormons looks more like we assume the latter, not the former. We Bible bash and then quixotically expect them to fall to their knees in abject penitence!

We've acted too much, too often like we simply need to "confront them with the truth" and correct their bad doctrine in order to evangelize them; too little, too seldom have we seriously acted like they might first need to *see* the truth—or more to the point, *experience* the truth—in working clothes, demonstrably incarnate, perhaps, for example, in the guise of a coach.

Much of this book is rooted in the notion that we are dealing with total persons who therefore have common ground with us in the wholeness of our humanity—persons often needing love more than "answers," respect more than competitive advantage, joy more than the thrill of winning at all costs, and the personal friendship of God more than a corrected theology of God. After all, as someone once asked me, are we here to evangelize Mormons or to evangelize *persons*, some of whom happen to be Mormons?

A second lesson is that *confrontation raises walls while incarnation lowers them.* Here in Utah, I've observed a strange inconsistency on the part of traditional Christians: we mouth truisms like "you can't argue anyone into the kingdom of God" and "we must win people, not arguments" as we continue confronting, arguing, and alienating LDS people with our polemical preachments! Generally, "Bible bash" evangelism with its heresy-hunting rationalism simply squashes the life out of relationships and builds walls, not bridges. What we say might sound to Mormon ears like intelligent news, critical news, or outright hostile news—never like "good news." But show them the love of Christ in a coach's jacket, show them an impassioned worshipper's tears, show them a free auto repair or give their house a paint job in the name of our Lord Jesus—and watch the walls begin to come down!

Third, *theology and right doctrine ought not be ignored but rather reassigned to the ripe moments of a relationship.* There's an appropriate time for everything under the sun, the sage of Ecclesiastes reminds us, and normally the time for biblical teachings (especially teachings that challenge

Mormon teachings) to be examined and discussed with an LDS person is *not* usually in the early moments of a relationship. The time isn't on the football field or in the student lounge with a Mormon we just met but in some moment down the road, maybe in your living room or a Sunday school class, when our friend begins asking how to understand the teachings of the Bible better. This then becomes a very important discipleship ministry—at the right time.

Fourth, *we should understand Mormons as a people group with their own culture.* They celebrate a history of their own and have a set of core values, a legendry, marriage practices, and other sensibilities and lifeways that give them a particular identity. I did not understand this beyond a passing nod when I first moved to Utah, so like many evangelicals who move here, I did lots of unnecessary bungling and offending. Others have had the same experience with LDS people in other places. Let me simply say that Mormons almost always personally feel a vital and sensitive connection to their whole "ethnic tradition." This connection is similar to the cultural identity felt by Italian Catholics or Arab Muslims—a very powerful personal attachment—and to communicate with LDS people, we must learn to respect them by taking this seriously and appreciatively (affirming the positive, yet not bashing the negative).

Fifth, *servanthood rather than mastery is the way of Jesus in dealing with people.* He came among us as one who serves, and just so, we should learn to take up our towels and serve others for his sake. I remember feeling in those early days in Utah how very impressed the Mormons might be if I could just show them I'd mastered their system of religious beliefs and also mastered the Bible, so naturally they'd end up trusting me to "enlighten" them. So, were they impressed, bowled over by my good, Bible-based arguments? Not in the least! As you've read above, such encounters just became one more alienating "Bible bash." But coaching their kids with love, feeding their dog for the weekend, singing at their husband's funeral, stage acting with excellence and integrity in their community theaters—these things, I learned, impressed them and opened doors for the gospel.

Jimi Pitts, a friend of mine who loves to present the gospel to Mormon people, has gone for several years to a big, famous annual pageant presented by the LDS Church in the small Utah town of Manti. Usually he's with a group of mostly young people. They would traditionally hand out tracts and talk to people gathered in the town for the event. The townsfolk did not take kindly to their presence, and one year they were not only harassed and persecuted (as they'd been for several years running), but the police even handcuffed and arrested Jimi. It was plain the community felt threatened and outraged as these traditional Christians stuck to their practices and kept handing out the tracts—quite admirably, I must say. Of course, very few gave them a serious hearing.

The next year after these incidents, they tried something very different. The group was made aware of a poor single mother living in town, a Mormon lady with five children, who needed her house painted. In the group came with their brushes, rollers, tarps, and paint that she got to pick out herself but the group paid for, as well as lots of hands and feet to do the job for her as a simple *gift of love*. Soon the word got out across the small Mormon community about what they'd done, and suddenly they were practically hailed as people who walked on water! Now it was as if they could do no wrong! Even though they continued to hand out tracts and talk to LDS passersby, they were now not only tolerated but in some cases even admired.

In the years to follow, the group continued painting homes of needy people, materials and labor all freely given, and fixing cars and doing other acts of service. The single mother became their friend, began to entrust her kids to them for tending, and one of her daughters even, as Jimi reported, "got saved!" More than one county law enforcement official later told Jimi with heartfelt apology, "We were wrong to do what we did to your group," and a good, open friendship has been formed with one of those officials in particular who is now open to their message. Their servanthood powerfully demonstrated how God's grace leads people to do good works and won for them many openings to proclaim the gospel to Mormons.

Finally, the sixth and perhaps most important lesson we can learn from our journey through this book is simply *truth must be experienced, not just expressed*. For many of my early years in Utah, I suffered from overconfidence in my powers of expression, acting as if people like my Mormon friend "Jason" would somehow "get the truth" from hearing my wise, informed, articulate words—even more so from hearing me quote words of Scripture. It was not to be. I needed to learn the writer's famous principle "show, don't tell" when communicating with LDS people, because they are a people of experience and drama and song and story. Philosophers and lawyers, as a rule, they're not, particularly in matters of religion and faith. Most often our LDS friends need to hear the music of the gospel before making sense of the lyrics. They need to "taste and see that the LORD is good" (Ps. 34:8).

Let me cap it all off with one of my very favorite anecdotes, to picture "the language of experience" in action. For my money at least, it's one of those little stories that says it all. It's a personal experience my friend and colleague Ken Mulholland had and told me about. As a background note, he tells me he used to recoil at the idea of praying with a Mormon because he thought it would imply he accepted the LDS claims to truth. This single encounter changed his mind and redirected his entire praxis.

It happened many years ago when Ken held a summer job in the lodge at Zion National Park, that dramatically beautiful "other Grand Canyon" located in southern Utah. Two of his co-workers were a traditional Christian we'll call Cindy and a committed Mormon lady we'll call Sally. Many times Ken and Sally would have lengthy "discussions" with robust arguments over Joseph Smith and Mormon doctrine and the Bible.

One evening the three of them took a drive through the park, and as the shadows lengthened and the golden-pink hues illumined the sky and deepened the gorgeous red of the canyon walls, all three were awestruck by the majestic beauty they beheld. As they continued their drive, Cindy piped up, "Why don't we stop and pray?" Ken swallowed hard and said okay despite his misgivings. So they pulled the car over and prayed, simply and intimately conversing with the Lord about their gratitude and wonder and perhaps other things Ken can't remember. When they finished, the other two noticed Sally had been moved to tears, although they didn't know why. Nothing was said about it as they resumed their drive.

The summer ended, the three went back to their respective homes in different parts of the country, and they fell out of contact with one another—until, that is, about one year later. Suddenly Sally showed up in Salt Lake City, Utah (not her home city or state), and got reacquainted with Ken. On meeting him again, she soon announced, "I've become a Christian."

Not only surprised and delighted but also curious, Ken asked, "Tell me, what did God use to open your eyes to the gospel of grace?" (Decoded version: "Which of my fine arguments was it that finally got through to you?")

Sally replied that her conversion had nothing to do with all those things they had argued about, none of which she could even remember, but something else had made a major impact on her that became a turning point. "It was that time we prayed together. At first I was offended by the intimacy with which you and Cindy addressed God. But I also had a second reaction: you two prayed as if God and you were on a first-name basis, but to me he was just 'Heavenly Father' way out there—and I wanted what you had." Now, that's a very classic, very telling tension many

LDS people feel in the midst of such experiences. But in that moment a hunger had surfaced inside Sally, a hunger for that freedom to have no fear in God's presence and to be on intimate "Abba, Father" terms with him.

Final Words

Many Mormon people who know you and me have this same hunger to know not just "Heavenly Father" but "Abba, Father," not just what my friend Judi calls (remembering her early years in Mormonism) "a two-dimensional cutout paper doll" Jesus Christ but the Jesus as real and personal as someone sitting in the chair across the table, looking deep into their eyes and talking with them, Friend to friend. *Every* human being has this hunger deep down, of course, to know their Creator on a first-name basis, but the cultural filter of Mormonism creates particular challenges for us in helping that hunger come to the surface and be filled.

In reaching the people group to which that culture belongs, the people called "Mormons," we face great opportunities just now because we're at a critical point in the history of traditional Christians relating to these people. Many, many LDS people are more open, more generous, more curious, even hungrier and thirstier than ever before to know the God who is in Jesus Christ. May we who know Jesus in a personal way take on a true missionary mind-set toward these people. May we seize the moment by learning the culture, loving the people, and speaking the Good News into their lives in a way that truly, fully, compellingly *sounds like good news!*

For Discussion and More

1. Share any stories you have of roadblocks former Mormons you know faced as they were in transition. Discuss what you can learn from these.

2. Describe and discuss what a "safe zone" for transitioning Mormons in a traditional Christian church might look like. What would need to characterize it to make it truly helpful to LDS people and to the congregation?
3. If you chair a Christian education committee in your church and you are charged with designing a curriculum for Mormons in transition, how might you state the purpose, objectives, topics, and methods you believe you should use?
4. What do you believe—and believe enough to practice—about praying with Mormons, and why? What did you learn from the story about "Cindy," " Sally," and Ken?
5. State a major lesson from this book that you've found especially significant and helpful for you in relating to and bringing the Good News to Mormon people. What do you think most traditional Christians need to know and do to most faithfully and effectively reach Mormons?

Appendix 1

The Articles of Faith of the Church of Jesus Christ of Latter-day Saints*

1. **We believe in God, the Eternal Father, and in His Son, Jesus Christ, and in the Holy Ghost.**
   These are seen as three "personages" who are physical (yes, even the Holy Ghost—composed of particles) and are separate "Gods," rather than having a common essence and unity of being as does the historic Christian Trinity.

2. **We believe that men will be punished for their own sins, and not for Adam's transgression.**
   There is no original sin, in other words. Besides, "Adam's transgression" was necessary for the first parents to be able to discern good from evil and for them to bear children; thus it is seen as a "fall upward."

3. **We believe that through the Atonement of Christ, all mankind may be saved, by obedience to the laws and ordinances of the Gospel.**
   This "Atonement" took place in Gethsemane as Jesus prayed and agonized. The verb "may" indicates this agony only opened the

*With Annotations by the Author

door for people to be "saved," rather than Jesus actually and fully saving them. So it secured not salvation but the opportunity for salvation if one performs sufficient "obedience" to what the LDS Church construes as "the laws and ordinances of the Gospel."

4. **We believe that the first principles and ordinances of the Gospel are: first, Faith in the Lord Jesus Christ; second, Repentance; third, Baptism by immersion for the remission of sins; fourth, Laying on of hands for the gift of the Holy Ghost.**
Notice these are "first" in importance, but also the first of many more principles and ordinances to follow. Repentance is a law to be repeatedly and conscientiously obeyed. The final two rituals must be performed by a Mormon male who holds priesthood authority, or they are not valid.

5. **We believe that a man must be called of God, by prophecy, and by the laying on of hands by those who are in authority, to preach the Gospel and administer in the ordinances thereof.**
This call is believed to be modeled after the call of Aaron to priesthood in the Old Testament. Again, only LDS authorities can pass this authority on through this ritual.

6. **We believe in the same organization that existed in the Primitive Church, namely, apostles, prophets, pastors, teachers, ev ingelists, and so forth.**
This structure of offices is seen to be holy because it is believed to be the same as the New Testament structure.

7. **We believe in the gift of tongues, prophecy, revelation, visions, healing, interpretation of tongues, and so forth.**
These manifestations, though infrequent, do occur in the LDS Church and are understood as experiential ways of validating and verifying its divine truth and power.

8. **We believe the Bible to be the word of God as far as it is translated correctly; we also believe the Book of Mormon to be the word of God.**
Notice the "as far as" qualifier for the Bible is absent in the case of the Book of Mormon. Translation errors are thought to have corrupted the text of the Bible, thus putting it under a cloud of suspicion as to how far it can be trusted, but the Book of Mormon

is believed to have escaped this problem. This claim to unadulterated purity for the Book of Mormon rests on the underlying claim that Joseph Smith translated the book (from golden plates) "by the gift and power of God" directly into English.

9. **We believe all that God has revealed, all that He does now reveal, and we believe that He will yet reveal many great and important things pertaining to the Kingdom of God.**
   "The heavens are open" is a popular LDS expression for this article. Implied is that the vehicle for God's special revelations to his Church (which is "the Kingdom of God") is not only scriptures but most importantly—and exclusively—the LDS prophet.

10. **We believe in the literal gathering of Israel and in the restoration of the Ten Tribes; that Zion (the New Jerusalem) will be built upon this the American continent; that Christ will reign personally upon the earth; and, that the earth will be renewed and receive its paradisiacal glory.**
    The "Ten Tribes" are interpreted to be the lost tribes of Israel who, in the Book of Mormon story, migrated by boat to the American continent and were the righteous, white-skinned Nephites from whom modern Anglo Mormons believe they are descended. Christ, the story says, visited the American peoples after his resurrection and will return to reign here at the end of time.

11. **We claim the privilege of worshipping Almighty God according to the dictates of our own conscience, and allow all men the same privilege, let them worship how, where, or what they may.**
    Separation of church and state is a very important core value and was especially so in early LDS history, when the Mormon community was radically different from the societal mainstream.

12. **We believe in being subject to kings, presidents, rulers, and magistrates, in obeying, honoring, and sustaining the law.**
    Today especially, Mormons take this quite seriously and are the most conservative and patriotic of citizens.

13. **We believe in being honest, true, chaste, benevolent, virtuous, and in doing good to all men; indeed, we may say that we follow the admonition of Paul—We believe all things, we hope all things, we have endured many things, and hope to be able**

to endure all things. If there is anything virtuous, lovely, or of good report or praiseworthy, we seek after these things.*
This strong moral idealism is of course a trademark of Mormon legacy and belief, and it becomes enacted legalistically through more detailed moral codes and communitarian practices (like the Word of Wisdom health code and the Church Welfare program to help the impoverished). Interestingly, included even in this central statement of doctrine is a reference—in the words about what they "endured" and "endure"—to their self-characterization as a persecuted people.

*Articles of faith are taken from The Church of Jesus Christ of Latter-day Saints, *Gospel Principles* (Salt Lake City: The Church of Jesus Christ of Latter-day Saints, 1997), 306–7.

Appendix 2

Changes in Mormon Doctrine

An Example

We need to appreciate a certain reality when we study the culture of any people group: to observe a culture is to observe a "moving target." Any culture constantly changes, usually in small increments, but the changes are real and significant because they tell us we can never fully get a fix on a culture, master it, and plan on it staying the same as our fixed understanding tells us. Here I'd like to give a tangible demonstration of one kind of small change we can observe over time in the doctrinal expression of LDS culture. It shows up in the piece of standard teaching literature called *Gospel Principles*, an official LDS Church–published handbook on Mormon beliefs.[1] We can track changes in wording and emphasis that occur in successive editions of this handbook since it was first published in 1978. We observe two very interesting things:

- The direction of the changes generally is moving, even if very subtly, away from the unorthodox, radically Mormon claims we do not find in the Bible.
- The subject matter of these changes is not just trivial but deals with central, crucial teachings of the LDS Church.

Let's look at three different items displaying these changes.

First, notice how there is a backing away from direct claims about the physicality of the "heavenly parents." In the 1978–1988 editions, the second chapter opens with these words: "Our spirits resemble our heavenly parents *although they have resurrected bodies*. We have inherited the potential to develop their divine qualities" (p. 9, emphasis mine). Since the 1992 edition, this passage reads, "Because we are spiritual children of our heavenly parents, we have inherited the potential to develop their divine qualities" (p. 11). The italicized expression has been removed—the reference, that is, to God and his wife having resurrected bodies.

Second, we see a backing away from the historic Mormon claim that humans can become "Gods." The 1978 edition says on page 290 (in chapter 47), "We can become *Gods* like our Heavenly Father" (emphasis mine). The parallel sentence in the 1997 edition and in the online edition today simply reads, "We can become like our Heavenly Father" (p. 302). This change is rather stunning because it is right at the core of LDS teaching and, if taken at face value, ends up modifying the statement to one with which in some respects a traditional Christian could agree!

Third, we see a softening of the extreme legalism in historic Mormon belief. The 1978–1988 editions have this sentence in chapter 46 (p. 285): "At the final judgement we will be assigned to the kingdom *we have earned*" (emphasis mine). The same passage, beginning with the 1992 edition, says, "At the Final Judgement we will be assigned to the kingdom for which we are prepared" (p. 297). The active verb used at first has become a passive verb and is not necessarily suggesting, in the later versions, obedience to laws and ordinances to earn divine favor.

These observations indicate a caveat we should all hold, namely, beware of thinking we can have all LDS teaching "nailed down" and that it will always be unorthodox and unbiblical. Even the textbook version may not remain the textbook version!

Appendix 3

Relating to Mormon Missionaries

A Model Story

People of traditional Christian faith often ask, "What do you think we should say to Mormon missionaries who knock at our door?" Of course, there's no one-size-fits-all answer to this, and that means there's every reason to seek the Spirit's wisdom for each particular encounter you may have with each particular pair of missionaries. Remember, these are persons, not just programmed entities with name badges.

So my counsel takes the form of storied adventures to provoke and encourage you in certain directions, rather than steps, formulas, or "recipes for success"—or, God forbid, weapons for your arsenal of arguments. Beyond the ideas I mentioned earlier, like asking for first names, giving a warm welcome and hospitality treats, and hearing their stories and telling yours, let me tell a story about how a faithful couple related to two Mormon missionaries. You've already met Paul and Jenna Murphy and read about their basic journey (chapter 7). Now look with me at this truly fascinating chapter in their lives.

It started when their son Alex was at a friend's house where two LDS missionary women called. In their introductions, they also met Alex and immediately asked if he was LDS. When he said no, they asked, "Can we come to your house and talk with your parents?" Alex said yes, knowing his dad and mom wouldn't mind—and he wanted to be polite to the missionaries. The two women showed up within a week.

In the first meeting, as introductions were made and everyone got on a first-name basis, the Murphys asked the two missionaries about their backgrounds and experience in the LDS Church, and right up front the Murphys told the missionaries that they were both formerly Mormons. Paul and Jenna made it clear to the young women that they were not prospects to join the LDS Church but would love to know the women better and hear what they had to present. The women were intrigued and asked why the Murphys had left the LDS Church. So each of them briefly told their stories; a bottom-line remark Paul made was, "The place we want to be is in the place of truth. Christ *is* the truth. I didn't find a relationship with Christ in the LDS Church, so I went to a Bible study."

Besides simply listening with respect and showing genuine interest in the missionaries, as well as telling their own stories in a nonconfrontational way when asked, the Murphys made two remarkable, winsome statements to them. Note these well, because they show a humility, a wisdom, and a gentleness that I find rare among traditional Christians in this situation. First they said, "We're not out to prove we're right and you're wrong, but our assumption is we *all* want to be in the place of truth." Second, they said, "So go ahead and give us your lessons. We need to learn."

What we need to notice here besides the words spoken by the Murphys is that these statements were not a ploy! They were honest and guileless in their sense of needing to hear what good things the Mormon missionaries would bring to the table. As Paul told me, "We've learned they have things to offer, despite issues of difference—for example, in the area of service to our neighbors, our church can learn from them!"

In weekly meetings over the following two months, the young women took the Murphys through their entire set of lessons. Paul and Jenna listened respectfully, asking questions and making statements when they felt it appropriate (yes, including points of disagreement), though always in a spirit of learning and humility.

Now came a turning point: all four agreed they really wanted to keep on meeting, even though the "fixed" agenda was finished. So the LDS women asked what they should do next, and the Murphys simply said, "Why don't we do a Bible study together?" The missionaries accepted the invitation, and they were off and running! Again, let me note this was not a ploy nor any kind of bait and switch: the "together" part was meant genuinely and embraced as such. They picked the book of Matthew to begin. One week the Murphys prepared and led the study, and the next week the LDS missionaries did it.

At first "the sisters" did not know what to expect, but soon they learned to love the fact that they were going to study the Bible more slowly than they had ever done—one chapter per week. In the process, they got to see how God had touched the Murphys and how God had touched the two of them. Yes, there were big walls up initially, but not as time went on. After Matthew, they started in Acts at the missionaries' request, and at this writing—eighteen months later—they are still studying it together with the currently assigned pair. Because LDS mission policy is to frequently switch the missionaries to different areas, they've talked with thirteen different missionaries. "Every time a new woman comes in," the Murphys say, "we suspend the normal Bible study agenda and ask questions about the new person's life. Then every person shares their story."

Here's the stunning part—the results of all the relationship building the Murphys did. One day as they met, one of the missionary women told Paul and Jenna about a very sensitive and painful thing in her life, which she had never confided to anyone else. She further said that after mustering enough courage, she had sent a letter to her mother to spill the news, but her mother had not responded, and now the young woman feared rejection. But the rules of LDS missionary work forbade her to call home except on two days every year (Christmas and Mother's Day). Paul said, "Well, the rules don't forbid *me* calling your mother. What's the number?" He placed the call, telling the mother how vulnerable and fearful her daughter was feeling over the letter, how much she needed to be reassured, and how she loved her mother. Mother and daughter were immediately connected through this compassionate mediation as the daughter overheard Paul's conversation with her mother. With a full and tender heart, the daughter was able to receive her mother's reassurance and love. The young sister missionary thanked the Murphys from the depths of her heart and never forgot their kindness—and I'm sure she never will.

As things turned out, she was reassigned to a different area for a while and then came back and will finish her mission meeting with the Murphys. She had formed a very close, enduring relationship to her "other family." Jenna says that even though it was common among Christians she knew to repudiate and denounce Mormons, she has overcome this by the grace of God and learned to love the missionaries.

When Christmas came along, this same young sister and her companion both said to the Murphys, "You're like our parents away from home. We're closer to you than to anyone else. Could we come and spend Christmas day with your family?" Paul and Jenna were overjoyed to be a family to them.

Recently one of the pair related to the Murphys that she had told her mother she wants to go to a Bible study when she gets back home. Her mother was a bit shocked and, as the missionary put it, "freaked out." In response, the missionary's rather pointed question to her mother was, "Tell me, Mom, how much have we learned about the Bible in the LDS Church?"

To cap off this vignette, we do well to notice the tone of the Murphys in dealing with LDS missionaries and sharing their journey out of Mormonism with them. It is not a tone of denouncing what the LDS Church does but of lamenting what it lacks. Coupled with it is a tone of genuine respect and teachability. As Paul stresses, "We have no bad things to say about the LDS Church. We simply say we never found Jesus Christ in the LDS Church."

This kind of persistent, compassionate relating is how the work of drawing Mormons—even Mormon missionaries—to the kingdom of God gets done. My exhortation would simply be that of the Lord Jesus: "Go and do likewise."

Notes

Chapter 2: At the Heart of "The Forgotten Sector"

1. Thom Hopler, *A World of Difference: Following Christ beyond Your Cultural Walls* (Downers Grove, IL: InterVarsity Press, 1981), 12–14.

2. Quoted in Clifford Geertz, *The Interpretation of Cultures: Selected Essays* (New York: Basic Books, 1973), 4–5.

3. Quoted in Adam Kuper, *Culture: The Anthropologist's Account* (Cambridge: Harvard University Press, 1999), 16–17.

4. Quoted in Ralph D. Winter and Steven C. Hawthorne, *Perspectives on the World Christian Movement: A Reader* (Pasadena, CA: William Carey Library, 1981), 508–9.

5. Stephen White, *Higher Authority* (New York: Signet, 1994), 32–35.

Chapter 3: Roots and Wings

1. Joseph Smith, *The* Pearl of Great Price*: Writings of Joseph Smith* (Salt Lake City: The Church of Jesus Christ of Latter-day Saints, 1973), 48, 2:16–20.

2. Salt Lake Theological Seminary, Bridges: Helping Mormons Discover God's Grace, Module 1, DVD (Salt Lake City: Salt Lake Theological Seminary, 2003).

3. Ibid.

Chapter 5: 101 Laboratory

1. Salt Lake Theological Seminary, Bridges: Helping Mormons Discover God's Grace, Module 4, DVD (Salt Lake City: Salt Lake Theological Seminary, 2003).

2. The Church of Jesus Christ of Latter-day Saints, *"Preach My Gospel": A Guide to Missionary Service* (Salt Lake City: The Church of Jesus Christ of Latter-day Saints, 2004), 31.

3. Ibid., 35.

4. Ibid., 52.

5. Ibid., 75.

Chapter 6: Mormons in Transition

1. Quoted in Winter and Hawthorne, *Perspectives*, 508–9.

2. Salt Lake Theological Seminary, Bridges: Helping Mormons Discover God's Grace, Module 5, DVD (Salt Lake City: Salt Lake Theological Seminary, 2003).

3. J. A. C. Redford, *Welcome All Wonders: A Composer's Journey* (Grand Rapids: Baker, 1997), 24–25.

4. Salt Lake Theological Seminary, Bridges: Helping Mormons Discover God's Grace, Module 3, DVD (Salt Lake City: Salt Lake Theological Seminary, 2003).

5. Ibid.

Chapter 7: Love It or Leave It

1. Stephen E. Robinson, *Believing Christ: The Parable of the Bicycle and Other Good News* (Salt Lake City: Deseret Book Co., 1992), 15–16.

2. Dallas Willard, "Spiritual Formation in Christ for the Whole Life and the Whole Person," at the conference "For All the Saints," Beeson Divinity School, Birmingham, AL, October 3, 2000.

Chapter 8: The Heart of the Matter

1. Penelope J. Stokes, *The Miracle of the Christmas Child* (Nashville: J. Countryman, 1999), 13, 100.

2. Juan Antonio Flores, "Turning My Life Around," *Liahona*, May 1998, 40.

3. Karen Backman, "The Best Gift," *Friend*, September 1988, 2.

4. Lynette Burke Hale, "Real Testimony," *Friend*, August 1993, 43.

5. Kenneth Mulholland, quoted in *Bridges: Helping Mormons Discover God's Grace, Facilitator's Training Guide* (Littleton, CO: Serendipity House, 2001), 86–87.

6. Thomas à Kempis, *The Imitation of Christ* (Nashville: Thomas Nelson, 1999), 2.

7. David Biglar, "A Most Bright, Earnest and Winsome Company: The Christian Teachers Come to Utah," at the conference "Models of

Ministry among Mormons," Salt Lake Theological Seminary, Salt Lake City, July 26, 2003.

8. Utah Lighthouse Ministries, "September 11th Massacre," *Salt Lake City Messenger*, May 2002, http://www.utlm.org/newsletters/no98. htm.

Chapter 9: Speaking Mormonese

1. Salt Lake Theological Seminary, Bridges: Helping Mormons Discover God's Grace, Module 4, DVD (Salt Lake City: Salt Lake Theological Seminary, 2003).

2. Ibid.

3. I am aware that most people refer to this as the parable of the prodigal son. I insist on the plural "sons" because both the younger and the older son were prodigal, and I believe this was a major point Jesus was making when he told the parable.

4. Salt Lake Theological Seminary, Bridges: Helping Mormons Discover God's Grace, Module 4, DVD (Salt Lake City: Salt Lake Theological Seminary, 2003).

5. Ibid.

6. Richard Foster, *The Celebration of Discipline: The Path to Spiritual Growth* (San Francisco: Harper & Row, 1988), 30–31.

Chapter 10: Concluding the Journey

1. Salt Lake Theological Seminary, Bridges: Helping Mormons Discover God's Grace, Module 5, DVD (Salt Lake City: Salt Lake Theological Seminary, 2003).

Appendix 2: Changes in Mormon Doctrine

1. The Church of Jesus Christ of Latter-day Saints, *Gospel Principles* (Salt Lake City: The Church of Jesus Christ of Latter-day Saints, 1997).

A Selective Glossary of LDS Terms

In dealing with LDS social structure and doctrinal discourse, we must remember there are distinctly Mormon terms used that untutored outsiders may not understand, as well as familiar terms (many from the Bible, for instance) that have distinctly Mormon definitions. For example, the first several times somebody mentioned a "stake house," I thought we were going out to eat; and by the way, did you know "Adam" used to be "Michael" and helped create the earth? The following glossary is adapted from "A Lexicon of LDS Vocabulary" by Dr. Jeff Silliman, Executive Presbyter, the Presbytery of Riverside, San Bernardino, California.

Aaronic Priesthood. The lower of the two divisions of the priesthood in the LDS Church. Joseph Smith and Oliver Cowdery claimed to receive the Aaronic Priesthood on May 15, 1829, from John the Baptist. This priesthood is for males twelve years of age and over. It includes (in ascending order) deacons, teachers, priests, and bishops (those in charge of wards). *See also* Melchizedek Priesthood.

Adam. The first man; the father of the human race. Before his earthly life, he was known as Michael. He led the righteous in the war in heaven. He helped create the earth.

Administer the sacrament. To bless the sacrament.

Administer to the sick. To anoint and bless the sick by the power of the priesthood.

Age of accountability. The age at which a person becomes responsible for his or her actions and may be baptized; in most cases, eight years old.

Altar. In Latter-day Saint temples today, a place where covenants are made and couples or families are sealed together for time and eternity.

Anoint. To place a few drops of oil on the head, usually as part of a priesthood blessing.

Apostasy. Turning away from or leaving the teachings of the LDS gospel. Also the Great Apostasy—the time between the death of the apostles and Joseph Smith's establishment of the LDS Church. Latter-day Saints believe that during this period of time the true Church was lost from the earth.

Apostle. A person called and appointed to be a special witness for Christ. An office in the Melchizedek Priesthood.

Articles of Faith. Thirteen statements written by the prophet Joseph Smith describing some of the basic teachings and ordinances of the Church of Jesus Christ of Latter-day Saints (see appendix 1).

Atonement. The suffering and death of Jesus Christ, through which resurrection is provided to all mortals and eternal life is offered to those who have faith in Christ and repent of their sins. When Adam sinned, he brought about temporal death and spiritual death. Temporal death is the separation of the spirit and the physical body. Spiritual death is separation from God. Because Jesus died and rose, the body and spirit are reunited in immortality. Immortality then comes as a free gift but does not determine where eternity will be spent. Eternal life spent with God is only achieved by obeying the fullness of the gospel law.

Authority. The right to function in certain capacities in the Church.

Baptism. Must be performed by an authorized member of the priesthood, by immersion, and is for those eight years old or older. Baptism is one of the requirements to enter the Celestial Kingdom.

Baptism for the dead. Baptism by immersion performed by a living person for one who is dead. This ordinance is performed in temples. Baptism is essential for all worthy people to become heirs of salvation in God's Kingdom.

Many people have not been given the opportunity to be baptized in their own lifetime due to accidents of time or geography. Therefore, to provide the opportunity for eternal life, the LDS Church accepts such responsibility and hopes to perform such a sacrament for every living soul entitled to receive it. All worthy baptized Mormons twelve years of age and over may be baptized for deceased non-Mormons. This is done by proxy and necessitates an extensive genealogical library so Mormons can discover the identity of their dead relatives.

Bible. One of the standard works of the LDS Church. It includes the Old and New Testaments and is the first revelation from God, but only one of many. In itself, the Bible does not contain sufficient information for salvation. It is to be understood only as correctly interpreted by proper LDS authority, as the Bible is believed to have been corrupted through the centuries. The King James Version is the only acceptable and complete English version of the Bible. To understand the King James Version from a Mormon perspective, Joseph Smith revealed the Inspired Version of the Bible (Joseph Smith's own translation).

Bishop. A man who has been ordained and set apart as the presiding high priest for a ward. He has responsibility for the temporal and spiritual well-being of all his ward members. He also presides over the Aaronic Priesthood.

Book of Mormon. One of the standard works of the LDS Church. It is an account of God's dealings with the people of the American continents from about 2,200 years before the birth of Jesus Christ to 421 years after his death. It was translated from gold plates by Joseph Smith and contains the fullness of the gospel.

Born in the covenant. Born to parents who have been sealed in the temple.

Branch. A developing ward.

Called. To be assigned a duty or position in the Church.

Celestial Kingdom. The highest kingdom of glory, where one is in the presence of Heavenly Father and Jesus Christ. Only those who have accepted LDS doctrines and ordinances will be assigned to the Celestial Kingdom. The Celestial Kingdom is the only place where Heavenly Father resides and governs. This kingdom is subdivided into three levels in descending order. The highest level is for those who have been obedient to the gospel and have been married in an LDS temple. No one goes into the highest level of the Celestial Kingdom single. The second level is for LDS people who are more active in the LDS Church positions but not involved in temple rituals. The lowest level is for those who received LDS baptism. Both the second and third levels serve those in the highest level.

Confirmation. An ordinance in which a person is confirmed a member of the Church of Jesus Christ of Latter-day Saints by the laying on of hands and is given the gift of the Holy Ghost. The ordinance is performed after baptism.

Council in heaven. The meeting in heaven in which Heavenly Father announced the plan of salvation and chose Jesus Christ as our redeemer.

Devil. A spirit son of God who rebelled against the Father and tried to destroy the agency (free will) of man. He is also known as Lucifer or Satan and is the author of sin.

Dispensation. A period of time in which truth from heaven is given to people on earth through prophets.

Doctrine and Covenants. One of the standard works of the LDS Church, containing revelations given to Joseph Smith and other latter-day presidents of the Church.

Endowment. A gift of power given through ordinances in the temple to worthy members of the Church. The endowment includes instructions about the plan of salvation.

Enduring to the end. Obedience to God's laws to the end of mortal life.

Eternal life. Another name for godhood and synonymous with exaltation; living eternally as God.

Eternal Progression. The concept that a person can progress through the three estates (premortal, mortal, post-mortal), eventually obtaining godhood.

Exaltation. The highest state of happiness and glory in the Celestial Kingdom; the culmination of Eternal Progression; the continuation of the family unit in eternity; the highest level of the Celestial Kingdom; obtaining godhood.

Fast offering. Contribution to the Church of the money or commodities saved by fasting for two consecutive meals.

Final judgment. The time when God assigns all people to their eternal destiny. This occurs at the end of earth history and determines where each person ends up in "post-judgment."

First judgment. Event occurring immediately after physical death in which all human beings go to either Paradise or spirit prison, where they are held until post-judgment.

First Presidency. A quorum that presides over the entire Church; made up of the president of the Church and his counselors.

Foreordination. Callings given by Heavenly Father to his children to come to earth at a specific time and place to help with his work in a particular way.

Full-tithe payer. A person who pays one-tenth of his or her annual increase to the Lord.

General Authority. Refers to the LDS leaders who have highest authority, including the First Presidency, the Council of the Twelve, the First and Second Councils of the Seventy, and the Presiding Bishopric.

Gentile. A person who does not belong to the chosen people. The scriptures use the word to mean (1) non-Israelites and (2) non-members of the Church of Jesus Christ of Latter-day Saints.

Gift of the Holy Ghost. The right, received by the laying on of hands, to enjoy the constant companionship of the Holy Ghost when we are worthy.

Gifts of the Spirit. Spiritual blessings given by God to those who are faithful to Jesus Christ.

God. Our Father in Heaven, the Father of Jesus Christ in the flesh and of the spirits of all humankind. God is an exalted man.

Godhead. Our Father in Heaven; his Son, Jesus Christ; and the Holy Ghost. These are three separate personages who form the highest ruling council. These are not the only divine beings, however. God the Father had a God, who had a God, and so on back through all eternity so far as we know. This concept has not been emphasized in LDS teaching lately, but the prophet Joseph Smith taught it, and the Church has not repudiated it.

Gospel (restored gospel). The plan of salvation, which embraces all that is necessary for us to be saved and exalted. It includes both unconditional and conditional elements.

Grace. Refers to God's unmerited gifts to humans. Grace is necessary, but not sufficient, for the salvation and exaltation of human beings.

Heavenly Father. The father of the spirits of all humankind. He is an exalted being with a body of flesh and bones.

Hell. That part of the spirit world where wicked spirits go following death to suffer for their sins while awaiting their eventual resurrection. After their resurrection, the great majority of these persons will pass into the Telestial Kingdom. Thus, for those who are heirs of some degree of salvation, hell has an end. However, those who have given themselves over wholly to satanic purposes will be cast into Outer Darkness following their judgment.

Holy Ghost. The third member of the Godhead; a personage of spirit. The Holy Ghost is separate from Heavenly Father and Jesus and different from the Holy Spirit. The Holy Ghost is a spirit person (no flesh and bones), can be in only one place at a time but can influence the world, and is the revealer and testifier of truth.

Holy Spirit. Heavenly Father's spirit and extended power—different from the Holy Ghost.

House of Israel. Natural or adopted descendants of the sons of Jacob, who was given the name "Israel" by the Lord.

Inspiration. Divine guidance that comes through the promptings of the Holy Ghost.

Israel. (1) The name given to Jacob of the Old Testament. (2) The name given to the descendants of Jacob's twelve sons. (3) The modern nation to which many Jews have gathered today.

Jack Mormon. A slang expression for an inactive Mormon.

Jesus Christ. The only begotten son of the Father in the flesh and the firstborn son in the spirit; our redeemer and savior. We are all spirit children of Heavenly Father; Jesus is Heavenly Father's eldest spirit child. He came to earth in spirit as Jehovah in the Old Testament. In this state he organized earth. He came to earth in body by being born to the virgin Mary. Jesus' death secured immortality (life after death) for all people and also secured the opportunity for spiritual progression/advancement by the forgiveness of sins. The quality of life achieved in immortality remains up to individuals and the free agency they exercise during their mortal existence.

Kingdom of God. The Church of Jesus Christ of Latter-day Saints on earth; also the Celestial Kingdom.

Line of authority. Every priesthood holder should be able to trace his "line of authority" back to Jesus Christ. This means he should know who ordained him and who ordained the person who ordained him, and so forth back to Joseph Smith, who was ordained by Peter, James, and John, who were ordained by Jesus Christ.

Marriage. Marriages performed in the temples are for the present and forever if the vows are kept. The highest level of the Celestial Kingdom is only for those who have been so sealed. As baptism is the gate to the Celestial Kingdom, celestial marriage is the gate to exaltation in the Celestial Kingdom.

Melchizedek Priesthood. Peter, James, and John restored the ancient Melchizedek Priesthood in June 1829 upon Joseph Smith and Oliver Cowdery. This priesthood includes, according to function, the offices of elder (men eighteen years and over who usually subsequently serve two years as a missionary for the LDS Church), Seventy, High Priest, Patriarch or Evangelist, and Apostle.

Mortal existence. Earthly existence in a body that is subject to death, also called the Second Estate. Human bodies are provided for worthy spirit children by physical childbirth. Life on earth is a testing time that requires all to be separated from Heavenly Father in order to prove that they will obey the gospel. Obtaining a human body is essential for spiritual advancement/Eternal Progression.

Nonmember. A person who is not a member of the Church of Jesus Christ of Latter-day Saints.

Ordinances. Sacred rites and ceremonies that are necessary for Eternal Progression; God's laws and commandments.

Outer Darkness. Also called the Second Death. This is the place to which Satan, unrighteous spirits, and extreme cases of apostasy such as Cain and Judas are sent following judgment.

Paradise. The part of the spirit world where righteous LDS people go immediately following death until the day of their resurrection and judgment, when they will be assigned to one of the three levels of the Celestial Kingdom.

Patriarchal blessing. An inspired blessing declaring a person's lineage and giving inspired counsel and insight about his or her life.

Pearl of Great Price. One of the standard works of the Church.

Plan of salvation. Our Heavenly Father's plan for his children by which they can overcome sin and death and gain eternal life. It includes all the Latter-day Saint laws and ordinances. Following the plan of salvation is the key to being exalted.

Post-judgment. Consists of the permanent assignments to the three kingdoms—Celestial, Terrestrial, and Telestial—and to Outer Darkness.

Post-mortal existence. The last stage of development in LDS theology. This final destiny consists of three parts: first judgment, final judgment, and post-judgment. Immediately after physical death, all human beings go to either Paradise or spirit prison where they are held until final judgment.

Premortal existence. The period between the birth of spirit children of Heavenly Father and their birth into mortal life. God the Father created spirit children (humans without bodies of flesh and bone yet with intelligence, free will, and experience). Spirit children advance to earth (the Second Estate) through righteous pre-earth existence.

Priesthood. The power and authority of God given to men on earth to act in all things for our salvation. There are two priesthoods: Melchizedek and Aaronic. Both are reserved for male members of the LDS Church and hold the only authority for ordination, baptism, and other essential ordinances.

Prophet. One who has been called of the Lord to be a special witness of the divinity of Jesus Christ. The Prophet refers to the president of the Church of Jesus Christ of Latter-day Saints.

Quorum. An organized unit of the priesthood.

Recommend. A certificate to identify people as members of the Church and to certify their worthiness to enter the temple and receive certain ordinances or blessings.

Relief Society. The main Latter-day Saint women's organization that meets every Sunday while the men meet in their priesthood quorums. The focus is more on self-improvement and being good homemakers and mothers than on theological matters.

Salvation. Inseparable connection of body and spirit brought about through the Savior's atonement and resurrection; eternal life. Christ's death brought release from the grave and gives universal immortality. The kingdom (Celestial, Terrestrial, or Telestial) to which one is resurrected depends upon one's spiritual and temporal activities on earth.

Scriptures. Words written and spoken by holy men of God when moved upon by the Holy Ghost. Mormon scriptures include the Bible, the Book of Mormon, the Doctrine and Covenants, and the Pearl of Great Price.

Sealing. An ordinance performed in the temple, eternally uniting a husband and wife or children and their parents.

Sin. Breaking the laws of God.

Sons of perdition. The spirit hosts of heaven who followed Lucifer. Also those who gain a perfect knowledge of the divinity of the Savior and then turn from him and follow Satan.

Spirit prison. The place where all non-LDS people go immediately following death. LDS missionaries come here from Paradise and preach the gospel. Those who respond positively progress toward the Celestial Kingdom, aided by LDS temple work on their behalf and by LDS people still living on this earth.

Spiritual death. Separation from the Spirit of God and from his presence.

Stake. A geographical group of wards.

Standard works. The volumes of scripture officially accepted by the LDS Church: King James Bible, Book of Mormon, Doctrine and Covenants, and Pearl of Great Price.

Telestial Kingdom. The lowest kingdom of heaven or glory. It is not visited by Heavenly Father or Jesus but only by the Holy Ghost. Those assigned to the Telestial Kingdom are dishonest, liars, sorcerers, adulterers, and whoremongers. It is also for those who have heard but rejected the restored gospel as taught by the LDS, including former members of the LDS Church.

Temple. A place of worship and prayer; the house of the Lord prepared and dedicated for sacred gospel ordinances.

Temple garments. There are two kinds of temple garments. The first are special garments only worn in the temple; the second are sacred undergarments worn at all times (which many Mormons feel give them supernatural protection). Only temple-worthy Mormons can wear temple garments.

Temple work. Sacred gospel ordinances performed in temples by the living for themselves and for those who are dead. These ordinances include baptisms, washings, anointings, endowments, marriages, and sealings.

Terrestrial Kingdom. The middle kingdom of heaven or glory. The Terrestrial Kingdom is only for those who have not heard the restored gospel as taught by the LDS or who have been good and honorable but blinded by the craftiness of men. Jesus will visit the Terrestrial Kingdom, but Heavenly Father will not.

Testify. To declare what one knows; to bear witness.

Testimony. Knowledge revealed by the Holy Ghost of the divinity of the Savior and of gospel truths; assurance of the truthfulness of Mormonism. It is the most important thing a Mormon can possess. Nearly every testimony consists of four parts: (1) Jesus is the true Son of God; (2) Joseph Smith was a true prophet of God; (3) the Book of Mormon is the true word of God; and (4) the Church of Jesus Christ of Latter-day Saints is the true Church of God. Personal testimony is received through feelings, not facts: it is a burning in the bosom and a feeling of peace and assurance given by the Holy Ghost.

Trinity. Latter-day Saints do not believe in the Trinity.

Visiting teachers. Women from the Relief Society who visit their assigned women on a monthly basis.

Ward. The smallest ecclesiastical unit of the LDS Church, equivalent to the local congregation. A developing ward is called a *branch*.

Word of Wisdom. A revelation concerning health practices given to Joseph Smith in 1833 in section 89 of the Doctrine and Covenants. It is a list of substances to indulge in or abstain from. Mormons must abstain from wine, strong drink, tobacco, etc.

Zion. The name given by the Lord to those who obey his laws; the name of the place where the righteous live.

Resources

Books

Bigler, David L. *Forgotten Kingdom: The Mormon Theocracy in the American West, 1847–1896*. Logan, UT: Utah State University Press, 1998.

Cares, Mark J. *Speaking the Truth in Love to Mormons*. 2nd ed. Milwaukee: WELS Outreach Resources, 1998.

The Church of Jesus Christ of Latter-day Saints. *Gospel Principles*. Salt Lake City: The Church of Jesus Christ of Latter-day Saints, 1997. (Also downloadable from the LDS Church website. See below.)

Ludlow, Daniel H., ed. *Encyclopedia of Mormonism*. Salt Lake City: Inforbases, Inc., A Bookcraft Company, 1990.

Millet, Robert L. *The Mormon Faith: A New Look at Christianity*. Salt Lake City: Deseret Book Co., 1998.

Ostling, Richard N., and Joan K. Ostling. *Mormon America: The Power and the Promise*. San Francisco: HarperCollins, 1999.

Redford, J. A. C. *Welcome All Wonders: A Composer's Journey*. Grand Rapids: Baker, 1997. (Available only from Salt Lake Theological Seminary. See below.)

Sorenson, John L. *Mormon Culture*. Salt Lake City: New Sage Books, 1997.

Taylor, Samuel W. *The Last Pioneer: John Taylor, a Mormon Prophet*. Salt Lake City: Signature Books, 1999.

———. *Nightfall at Nauvoo*. New York: Macmillan, 1971.

———. *Rocky Mountain Empire: The Latter-day Saints Today*. New York: Macmillan, 1978.

DVDs/Videos

Brigham City. DVD. Directed by Richard Dutcher. Provo, UT: Zion Films, 2001.

God's Army. DVD. Directed by Richard Dutcher. Provo, UT: Zion Films, 2000.

Intellectual Reserve, Inc. Video. *Legacy*. Salt Lake City: Intellectual Reserve, 2000.

The R. M. DVD. Directed by Kirby Heyborne. Orem, UT: Halestorm Entertainment, 2003.

Salt Lake Theological Seminary. Bridges: Helping Mormons Discover God's Grace. DVD, video. Salt Lake City: Salt Lake Theological Seminary, 2000.

The Singles Ward. DVD. Directed by Kirby Heyborne. Orem, UT: Halestorm Entertainment, 2001.

Websites

The Church of Jesus Christ of Latter-day Saints: www.lds.org.

Salt Lake Theological Seminary (699 E. South Temple, Salt Lake City, UT 84102; 1-888-809-1265): www.slts.edu.

David Livingstone Rowe serves as a missionary with Mission to the Americas (Denver) in strategic partnership with Salt Lake Theological Seminary, where he is a professor and dean of spiritual life. He teaches courses in homiletics/communication, spiritual formation, cross-cultural ministry, worship theology, and biblical studies. He holds B.A. (Rutgers University) and M.Div. (Denver Seminary) degrees, as well as M.S. and Ph.D. degrees in communication (University of Utah). He and his wife, Hazel, live in Salt Lake City and are the parents of three children. Beyond his family and Jesus, Dave's special loves are incendiary worship, fine cuisine, acoustic music, elegant discourse, and sheer grace.